AUTOMATA GALLERY

CH00823451

EXAMPLE 5: THE OWL AND THE PUSSYCAT

The Owl and the Pussy-Cat
went to sea
In a beautiful pea-green boat.

They took some honey,
and plenty of money,
Wrapped up in a
five-pound note.

The idea for the design of this automaton came from the first lines of the well-known poem 'The Owl and the Pussy-Cat', written by Edward Lear in 1871.

There is no turning action in the mechanism which simply uses a system of pushrods to operate the oars.

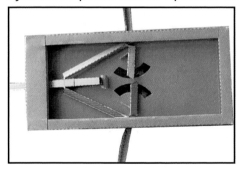

The mechanism can be clearly seen by turning the model upside-down, breaking the rule that it is generally unusual to hide, or keep secret, any automaton mechanism. As an amusing extra the movement of the pushrod also causes the cat's tail to move in time with the oars.

This openness about the mechanism is exactly the reverse of the situation with conjuring tricks, where secrets are normally carefully guarded and seldom ever revealed to the audience.

This automaton illustrates another rich seam of material that might suggest a theme for a model, that of well-known poems, verses, riddles or sayings. However, such phrases or words do need to be well-known. There does have to be a resonance and a response in the mind of the observer as the movement takes place.

EXAMPLE 6: THE WEIGHT OF BUREA

This example is a good illustration of how automata can also be used to make a political statement, in much the same way as cartoons in so many newspapers do. It was originally called 'Unemployment Policy' and was designed to comment on a new policy of the German Government which the designer thought was unfairly penalising the unemployed. By showing a large arm beating the unemployed person on the head and hammering him into the ground, he is suggesting in a vivid way that the Government is picking on the weakest members of society to solve its problems.

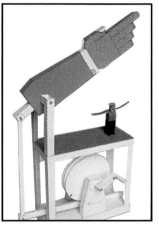
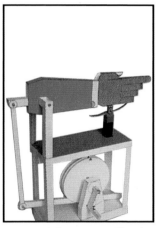

It was an appropriate comment for a particular piece of law-making in Germany, but in an English context the same automaton but with a different name could also be made to make a different political statement. For instance, according to the point of view of the designer, the arm could be seen to represent either the weight of new anti-trade-union laws bearing down on the workers or the weight of government bureaucracy bearing down on the small businessman.

The title above is a possible one in English but another might have been 'The Long Arm of the Law'. Although this phrase is usually used to refer to the police who supposedly never forget a crime, it could well be used to imply that there are too many laws for the well-being of society. For this kind of political statement to be effective it must be topical and of sufficient general interest to awake a response in a large enough audience.

AUTOMATA GALLERY

EXAMPLE 7: OFF ROAD

This automaton illustrates a type where the interest is in the clever mimicking of a particular kind of motion. Most of us have at some time seen a motorcyclist or a mountain biker slowly passing along a rough track and trying to manoeuvre his machine over a serious bump or obstruction. The technique is to balance carefully while lifting and bouncing first the front wheel and then the back one over the obstacle.

The designer makes use of a series of cranks and levers to produce this kind of movement realistically while the handle is being turned at a steady speed. However, still more realism is needed and so the set of the head of the rider and the serious expression on his face help to confirm the illusion. We can see clearly that he is concentrating on a difficult task. Such a combination of movement and the modelling is an important ingredient for a successful automaton.

EXAMPLE 8: THE OLD MAN AND THE SEA

A well-modelled sailor, the motion of a choppy sea and a title from a short story by Ernest Hemingway combine to make a fine automaton.

EXAMPLE 9: HOPPING SHEEP

There is a time in the spring when new-born lambs skip and hop in the sunshine and this was the inspiration that led to this delightful automaton. The modelling of these sheep is very simple indeed but is totally adequate for its purpose.

Wind the handle at a steady speed and the two adult sheep hop up and down in a rather adult way, just once for every turn. However at the same time, the little lamb behaves in a much more youthful, joyful and spring-like way, making this a most pleasing model to operate. Each of the sheep is driven by its own cam, all on a single shaft.

EXAMPLE 10: EWE BOAT

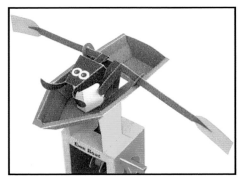

This automaton depends for its success on two things, a simple wordplay (Uboat = Eweboat) and the fact that for some reason sheep are seen by most people to be amusing!

While working on the model the designer visited Lake Windermere in Cumbria to watch a variety of people rowing boats on the lake. He wanted to see how the movement of their heads synchronised with the motion of the oars. He then adjusted the mechanism until he was able to mimic in his model a similar synchronisation of the sheep's head with the oars. Such care and attention to detail is important for any designer of automata because it brings a touch of reality to the models which is unconsciously recognised and appreciated by the observer. A good automaton speaks to its audience on several levels.

AUTOMATA GALLERY

EXAMPLE 11: THE SHADOOF

This automaton was inspired by a visit to Egypt and can be best regarded as a moving three-dimensional picture. The figure and the decoration were suggested by images from surviving ancient Egyptian wall paintings. The mechanism uses a crankshaft to replicate the repetitive action necessary to draw water from the waterways to irrigate the farmer's crops.

Note that small pieces of cocktail stick have been used for many of the pivots in this model. To maintain the rather realistic impression that this scene presents it was very important that the pivots were inconspicuous, something that would be difficult to achieve solely in paper.

Notice also how the rope operates the man's hands while giving the impression that it is he who is pulling the rope.

EXAMPLE 12: THE MYSTERY OF THE PYRAMIDS

This is another model which was inspired by ancient Egypt. This time it is not at all realistic!

It may be a great mystery how the pyramids were built but part of the delight in the automaton is that everyone knows that this is not the technique which was used.

This automaton is actually operated by a handle on the far side of the wheel but gives the impression that the hands of the mason are doing the turning. As the wheel is rotated, a series of linked levers slowly raises and lowers the little pyramid. Notice once again the use of cocktail stick pivots in this model which is realistic in the artistic sense but 'Heath Robinsonish' is the mechanical sense. Heath Robinson was a British artist and designer of complicated and often absurd machines that did not achieve very much. He died in 1944 but would have delighted in the frivolity and the absurd nature of the automata that have been designed since then.

TO SUM UP

This selection of a dozen paper automata by three different designers illustrates just a few of the concepts which have motivated and inspired them. It is hoped these examples will suggest methods for you to use to search out suitable topics, sayings, jokes or themes to use as an idea for your own designs.

The remainder of this book is devoted to a collection of useful paper engineering techniques that can be used to express those ideas. The wonder and delight of paper engineering is that it is so easy to experiment and so easy to invent new techniques. Rather like learning a language, once the basic grammar has been mastered, the number of possibilities for using that grammar is endless.

Now for the techniques!

WORKING WITH PAPER

A VERSATILE MATERIAL

Paper is a wonderfully versatile material and can easily be obtained in a wide range of thicknesses. For these models a thickness of 160gsm is probably about right and certainly it is generally not necessary to go above 200gsm. Although it is called the 'thickness', it is actually classified in terms of the weight in grams per square metre. It is certainly an easier measure to use than to have to obtain a precision micrometer to measure the thickness directly. Although certain papers of the same 'grammage' are thicker or thinner than others this is not generally of any significance in model-making work.

The secret of strength and stability of paper models lies in the folding. Once a piece of paper has a fold in it, then it is much stronger and stiffer.

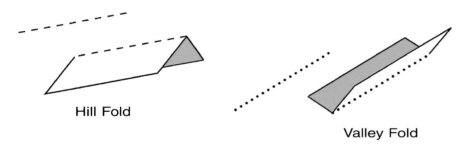

Hill Fold

Valley Fold

There are only two ways that it can be folded, away from you to make a hill fold and towards you to make a valley fold. The symbols used to represent these folds are not standard and different designers use different symbols. In this book we use the symbols shown above.

SCORING

It is most important that the paper is folded cleanly at every place where it needs to be folded and the best way to achieve this is to slightly compress the paper fibres by pressing on the fold lines with a ball-point pen which has run out of ink. This technique produces clean edges which are exactly in their intended places.

Where the fold lines are straight, as in most cases they will be, it is best to use a ruler or straight edge to guide the ball-point pen. Press on some clean card or perhaps on a cutting mat.

A CONVINCING DEMONSTRATION

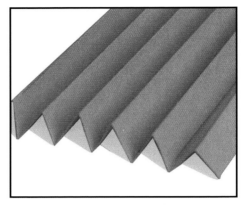

Here is an illustration of a classic experiment. It shows in a convincing fashion the strength that alternate hill and valley folds can impart to paper. Often the experiment is done with a real folded banknote because everyone is familiar with how thin and how flexible a normal banknote is. However, when folded into a concertina shape, it then becomes sufficiently strong and rigid to easily support a glass of water.

CUTTING OUT

A pair of scissors is perhaps the simplest way to cut out most of the parts of a paper automation, although it can sometimes be difficult to cut out clean holes and slots. An X-ACTO knife is very helpful for holes and slots and some people prefer to use the X-ACTO and a steel rule for everything. A hole punch can also be a useful tool in certain circumstances. It gives a clean hole but is difficult to position. However, on balance most people prefer to work with a combination, picking the most convenient tool for the job in hand.

TYPE OF GLUE

The choice of glue for automata making is an interesting one and there will be many opinions on what is best. Usually a spirit or petroleum based glue is more satisfactory for paper models than a water based one. Less time is needed for drying out and the risk of wrinkles developing is much reduced. We recommend UHU, especially the gel version, but there are others which are available and a little experimentation will soon uncover a suitable glue for your purposes.

14 Ingenious Automata, and More

PAPER MODELS THAT MOVE

Walter Ruffler

Dover Publications, Inc.
Mineola, New York

Acknowledgements

Rob Ives: Mexican Peck (p2), Hopping Sheep (p4&13), Ewe Boat (p4), Motley Man (p20), Pecking Hen (p20)

Rob Ives was a school teacher for many years and started to design paper automata as a hobby. Some of them were designed as kits and are now produced and marketed under the name 'Flying Pig.' He lives in Cumbria and now works full-time on his designs.

Magdalen Bear: The Owl & the Pussycat (p3), Busy Buzzy Bees (p19), Blue Footed Booby (p20), Noah's Ark (p20)

Magdalen Bear trained at the Glasgow School of Art and first took up a career as a textile designer. Later she came to specialise in graphic design and has tended to concentrate on paper models and 3D paper reliefs.

Copyright

Copyright © 2010 by Walter Ruffler
All rights reserved.

Bibliographical Note

Paper Models That Move: 14 Ingenious Automata, and More is a new work, first published by Dover Publications, Inc., in 2010.

International Standard Book Number

ISBN-13: 978-0-486-47793-0
ISBN-10: 0-486-47793-2

Manufactured in China by RR Donnelley
47793204   2019
www.doverpublications.com

CONTENTS

INTRODUCTION   IV

AUTOMATA GALLERY   1

WORKING WITH PAPER   6

SHAFTS, STRUTS & PUSHRODS   8

LEVERS, FULCRUMS & HINGES   10

CAMS & CRANKSHAFTS   12

CRANK SLIDERS   14

LINKAGES & JOINTS   15

FRICTION DRIVES & GEARWHEELS   16

LIMITING MOVEMENT   18

POWER SOURCES   20

MODELLING   22

THE FOURTEEN WORKING MECHANISMS   25

   INSTRUCTIONS   25

   MODELS   45

THE AUTHOR   108

INTRODUCTION

Working automata models do not need to be taken too seriously! They are usually made simply to appeal to our sense of fun and frivolity. Regard them as three-dimensional moving jokes which can be appreciated and enjoyed on at least two levels. Firstly, there is the pleasure of a smooth-turning movement acting to produce a vivid and graphic 'happening' which communicates an idea. Secondly, there is the pleasure of understanding and appreciating how such a mechanism works and how the required movement or combination of movements has been achieved by the designer.

Splendid working automata have been and can be made in many different materials or combinations of them such as wood, metal, fabrics, plastics and even ropes or cords. For such automata the most appropriate material is chosen for each purpose, metal for its strength, wood for its warmth and both fabrics and plastics for colours and light-weight coverings. Some automata use cords, ropes, wires or strings where there is a need only to pull, whereas wood and metal and sometimes plastic struts are used both to push and to pull. To make such automata often requires the use of a well fitted-out workshop and considerable skill with a variety of tools. Quite often the materials required are expensive to buy and difficult to obtain in small quantities. For an established designer working to a brief and to a contract, this is not a problem but it does deter those who would like to try their hands at this creative and rather addictive activity.

This book concerns itself solely with the skills and techniques needed to make working automata in paper, ideally paper alone. Paper is a wonderfully versatile material to work with. It can be cut, glued or folded with ease. Holes can be cut or punched in it and it can easily be decorated with paint or printed with colours, drawings or even photographs. Paper can be folded or concertina'd into structures of surprising strength and it is also readily available in a variety of beautiful colours. Nor is paper expensive and the tools needed to work with it are very modest and easily available. Perhaps all you need is a pair of scissors, a craft knife, a tube of glue, a ruler and a ball-point pen which has run out of ink.

Let us start to get serious about frivolity!

AUTOMATA GALLERY

THE IMPORTANCE OF A GOOD CONCEPT

Successful automata have some action or property which awakens a sense of recognition or 'rightness' in the mind of the observer. They are largely made for adults and not just for children but are undoubtedly things which parents and grandparents really like to show to children. This means that to a large extent the concept must first appeal to the adult. A child may find it sufficient that something simply goes round and round but this is not satisfying enough for most adults. What reason is sufficient is not easy to explain but it is easy to recognise it when we see it.

The first part of the book is therefore a gallery of twelve successful automata together with comments about them. This undoubtedly has its dangers. Comedians well know that it is very unwise to try to explain a joke because the humour in it immediately disappears. In a similar fashion it is rather dangerous to try to explain the idea behind an automaton. If it is not obvious, then the concept has failed! However this is a handbook of paper automata and a very important part of the design is the notion that it expresses.

EXAMPLE 1: SILENT NIGHT

The idea here is that an up to date Santa Claus might abandon his traditional sleigh drawn by reindeer and deliver his presents to children by motorcycle. When the handle is rotated, the motion suggests a rather frenetic and worried man intent on his task, not the traditional image of a jolly Father Christmas.

The title is also a good one. The mental image of the 'Silent Night' or 'Stille Nacht' of the original German carol, now so very well-known across the world for its stillness and charm, contrasts splendidly with the image and movement of a noisy motorcycle in a hurry. Will the children get their presents on time?

EXAMPLE 2: COMPUTER CONTROL

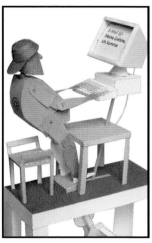

This automaton tries to convey something of the frustration of computer users when their computers crash at some vital moment. Most of us are only too aware of those desperate occasions when we realise that it is far too long since we last saved our work!

The name 'computer control' is a good one because it has a nice double meaning and one of which is only apparent when the handle is turned. Usually when a process is 'computer controlled' it is expected to work smoothly and accurately time after time. Generally this is exactly what happens. However, we all of us have in our heads images of mad computers going out of control and causing problems. Of course this image no doubt comes from science fiction films and TV programmes that we have seen, but also in real life most of us have been caught out from time to time when a malfunctioning computer will not let us open a 'computer controlled' door or let us start our 'computer controlled' cars or exit from a 'computer controlled' car park.

How can a moving paper model comment on these frustrations? In fact quite successfully and unexpectedly. Our computer operator sits calmly working at his desk until the handle is turned. The computer then crashes but not in the passive way that a real computer does. It rises off its stand and hauls the operator up with it. A most unexpected event. It is indeed the computer that is in control!

AUTOMATA GALLERY

EXAMPLE 3: MEXICAN PECK

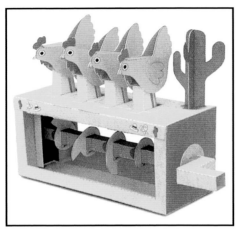

This automaton makes an amusing reference to the 'Mexican Wave' which can some-times be seen at sporting events when nothing very much is happening in the arena. Sections of the crowd stand up and raise their arms in turn, so giving the impression of a wave travelling around the ground.

The designer's idea was to suggest this activity by getting some chickens to peck the ground in sequence. He had an interesting judge-ment to make: to have sufficient chickens to make a wave but not so many that the paper engineering became tedious. His decision was to use four for his kit although he has made longer ones with up to eight chickens for exhibition purposes.

It is a simple and amusing concept which only requires a series of cams set to operate at different times as the axle or shaft is rotated to make it work. It does give a clear impression of a trav-elling wave.

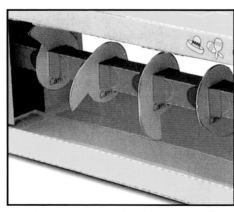

Another simple point is the use of a single cactus and a desert yellow colour to reinforce and suggest the idea of Mexico. That too is a simple visual joke because there is nothing at all especially Mexican about a chicken pecking the ground.

EXAMPLE 4: WIMBLEDON

The delightful idea is that of the twisting and turning back of heads as three members of an interested crowd watch an exciting rally at a major tennis tournament. The choice of the name is also important. It could well be that the best known world tennis tournament is Wimbledon but more important than that, it is a name associated with tennis. A title like 'US Open' or 'French Open' or even 'Grand Slam' could equally apply to other sports and the instant recognition would be lost.

This automaton also makes use of a very interesting and ingen-ious mechanism, using friction wheels. It is fully described on page 16.

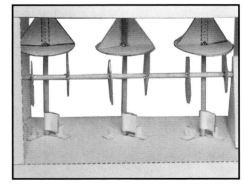

Sport is one of the most common shared experiences today and it offers a rich source of possible subjects and movements for automata. From golfers to skiers to sailors to windsurfers, they all offer some distinctive movements and events which can be tapped into. What about Switzerland, a landlocked country, winning the greatest sailing trophy, the America's Cup!

WORKING WITH PAPER

STRENGTH FROM FLAPS

Whenever a flap is glued to another surface the paper immediately becomes twice as thick over that area. In addition the layer of glue itself adds further strength to the join. Strong as it may seem after a few minutes when the glue has set, this join will continue to strengthen for at least another 12 hours. Patience is a virtue especially for parts which will take the strain of movement. Leaving the model until the next day is often a sound strategy.

STRENGTH FROM THREE-WAY CORNERS

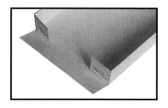

Simple flaps like those in this model produce firm right-angle corners and considerably add strength to the kind of tray-shapes often used for bases and lids. The edges of the flaps can be made to fit neatly against the folded end.

USING MITRES

However, most models need surfaces to meet in other ways and two flaps may meet on a receiving surface. In that case it is best to 'mitre' them, that is to share the angle available equally between them. For example, if a corner is a right angle, then the two flaps should be cut at about 44° each. The 2° difference being just enough to ensure a tightish fit without risking overlap.

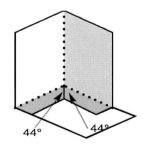

Always avoid overlaps, otherwise there are three thicknesses of paper and a rather ugly finish. Any small gap which remains will fill with glue and scarcely show.

DESIGN CONSIDERATIONS

As your experience in making paper models grows you will be able to find ways of folding and glueing which impart the maximum amount of strength and efficiency to a component while using the least amount of paper and glue. Always think also of how to reduce the number of separate pieces. If two pieces are to be glued edge to edge, could they perhaps be made from a single piece, folded in the appropriate place?

BASES AND FRAMEWORKS

This is a typical base to use for paper automata. It is easy to construct with a minimum of paper and yet the eight three-way right-angle corners give it a satisfactory rigidity. Since in general the 'works' or the mechanism of an automaton should be clearly visible, some variation on this kind of structure is at least a good starting point.

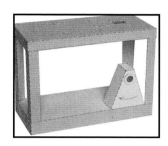

MAKING SHAFT SUPPORTS

Since most automata mechanisms include turning shafts there needs to be an efficient and simple way of making supports to hold them. A depth of about a centimetre is sufficient for a free-standing shaft and a circular hole is all that is needed as a bearing.

For the demonstration models in this book the shape chosen is a trapezium. It has advantages and seems a good compromise between various requirements. However, there are alternatives and their advantages and disadvantages are discussed below.

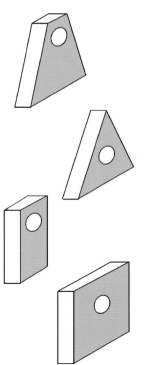

A triangle is a very strong shape and is easy to make. However, for there to be sufficient width of paper remaining around the hole, the hole has to be rather low. For the demonstration models this was an important factor and was why the trapezium was chosen instead.

A rectangular box is another simple shape but the area available for glueing to the base is relatively small and this may be a source of weakness.

Making the box wider to avoid this problem consumes rather a lot of paper. It is a question of keeping an open mind and looking for the best compromise for your purpose.

SHAFTS, STRUTS & PUSHRODS

RODS OF SQUARE CROSS SECTION

Whether they are called shafts, struts, pushrods or simply rods all these components are essentially the same and they can all be made the same way. The difference in names is due to the use to which they are put, not to their construction. The word 'shaft' is used for rods which rotate, the word 'strut' is used for rods which form fixed parts of the automaton and the word 'pushrod' is used for rods which move up and down in a single direction.

The most satisfactory cross-section for such paper rods is a square one. A square is not an intrinsically strong shape but it can be greatly strengthened by dividing it into two triangles by the addition of an internal diagonal. There is a very simple net which produces the outline and its diagonal. This design doubles the thickness of two sides of the square and is a very satisfactory one to use.

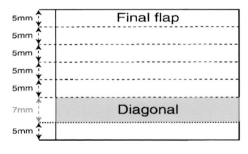

For maximum strength the diagonal should be straight and not bow at all. Ignoring the thickness of the paper, the length of the diagonal should be about 1.4 times the length of the side. However, the thickness of the card does matter and you will need to experiment with the paper you are to use. If after a trial you find that the diagonal does bow, then slightly reduce its width. You may need also to slightly increase the width of the final flap. The measurements above produce rods which are very strong and easy to use, and once you have got the widths right for your own paper you will be able to use the same measurements over and over again.

Amazingly, a square shaft of this design will rotate perfectly smoothly within a circular hole, thus making a simple and long lasting paper bearing.

BEARINGS FOR TURNING

Once the hole is cut, run a pencil around it to smooth out any rough edges and then the shaft will turn well, bedding itself in after a few turns. For a 5mm wide shaft a hole with a diameter of 7 or 8 mm is about right, but test this using the actual paper. If the hole proves to be not quite large enough insert a pencil or a suitable plastic tool and rotate it gently.

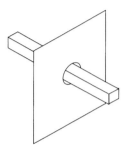
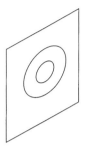

If extra strength is desired then it is a simple matter to add one or more reinforcing rings around the hole. Aesthetics may suggest that reinforcing rings are better out of sight and behind. As with a single thickness hole it is a good idea to run a pencil or another tool around the hole to smooth the edges before inserting the shaft for the first time.

GLUEING RODS TOGETHER

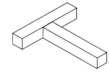
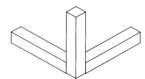
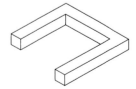

Rods of square cross-section have another distinct advantage in paper engineering. They are very easy to glue together to make larger and more complicated assemblies. The demonstration models illustrate a selection of different ways to join such rods together but no doubt you will be able to discover new ways of your own, depending on what you are trying to achieve. Once the glue is truly set, these units become surprisingly strong.

SHAFTS, STRUTS & PUSHRODS

RODS OF TRIANGULAR CROSS-SECTION

Any shape of triangle is intrinsically strong but there are two special triangles which are most likely to be used in the context of paper automata models. There is both simplicity and symmetry if the cross-section of a triangular rod is either an equilateral triangle or a right-angled isosceles triangle. Any other shape of triangular cross section is likely to be used in only the most exceptional of circumstances. All rods of triangular cross-section can be conveniently made from a scored rectangle of paper.

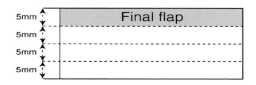

5mm	Final flap
5mm	
5mm	
5mm	

If the cross-section is to be equilateral, all four strips should theoretically be of the same width. However, if the paper is thick and the size of the strut makes it necessary to take notice of that thickness, then it is the inside strip which needs to be a little narrower.

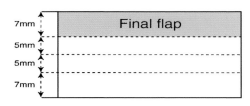

7mm	Final flap
5mm	
5mm	
7mm	

For the right-angled triangle, the hypotenuse should be 1.4 times the shorter sides. It is probably best if it is the hypotenuse that is the side which is of double thickness.

RODS OF CIRCULAR CROSS-SECTION

It is possible to make paper rods of circular cross-section by spreading glue on one side of a rectangle of paper and then rolling it up tightly into a cylinder. However, such rods are difficult to join together and surprisingly easy to dent or damage. They are not recommended except in very special circumstances.

RODS BY SIMPLE FOLDING

Sometimes a simple score and fold along its length is all that is needed to make a two-sided rod which will provide sufficient strength for a particular situation. For example the two struts in the stork automaton on page 13 that cause the wings to flap are made in just this extremely simple way.

COCKTAIL AND KEBAB STICKS

Rather than confining themselves to paper struts with their inherent bulkiness, some designers prefer in certain situations to make use of cocktail sticks, kebab sticks or even lengths of wooden dowelling rods which are easily available in various diameters from DIY stores.

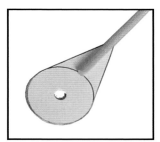

The biggest problem with using such wooden components lies in the difficulty of glueing them satisfactorily to the paper parts of the model. Because a circular surface does not glue easily to a flat one, such assemblies often work loose in use. For this reason some designers swear by the spent match as a convenient source of wooden strength for small joints. Its greatest advantage is its square cross-section.

It is also possible to make effective gear-wheels of cocktail sticks and two of them will even mesh at right angles and so give the possibility of a change of direction and speed. A layer of thin paper glued over the sticks and pressed down firmly between them will help to attach them permanently to the axle.

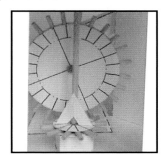

LEVERS, FULCRUMS & HINGES

THE THREE TYPES OF LEVERS

A certain understanding of the principles of levers is essential for a paper automata designer. Levers offer the designer a method of transferring actions and movements to a different location and a way of increasing or reducing the size of such movements. They were first classified by the great Greek mathematician, physicist and engineer Archimedes (287-212 BC) into three types, depending on the relative positions of the effort, the action and the fulcrum (the pivoting point). The force required to move the lever, quite often the input by a person, is called the 'effort'. The point at which this effort is applied is called the 'effort point'. The result of this effort is an action or movement at another location. In real engineering, it is usual to describe this action as the 'load' but in paper engineering it seems more appropriate to use the word 'action' and the place where it happens, the 'action point'.

An 'effort' in one place produces an 'action' in another place.

LEVERS OF THE FIRST TYPE:

The effort point and the action point lie on opposite sides of the fulcrum.

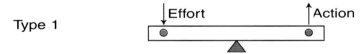

Type 1

A lever of the first type can be used to increase or reduce the size of a movement, according to which of the two arms is longer.

EXAMPLE A: The effort arm is shorter than the action arm.

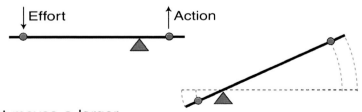

The action point moves a larger distance than the effort point and in the opposite direction.

EXAMPLE B: The effort arm is longer than the action arm.

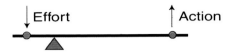

The action point moves a smaller distance than the effort point and in the opposite direction.

Note that both ends move on arcs of circles centred on the fulcrum. So do the effort and action points. These points can be at the ends of the lever or not. This depends on other considerations in the design.

USING TYPE 1 LEVERS

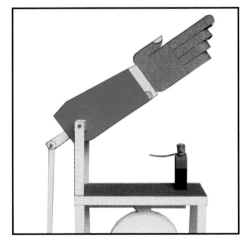

In order that the hand crashes overwhelmingly down on the poor unfortunate below, its rate of movement has to be increased. It therefore uses a lever like Example A where the effort arm is much shorter than the action arm. A small movement at the effort point gives a big movement of the hand. In contrast, although the Shadoof uses the same type of lever, the fulcrum lies more centrally and the effect is much more measured and gentle. The proportions on either side of the fulcrum in each case were chosen carefully to get the required effect.

LEVERS, FULCRUMS & HINGES

LEVERS OF THE THIRD TYPE

The effort point and the action point lie on the same sides of the fulcrum with the effort point nearer to the fulcrum.

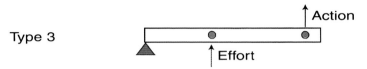

A lever of the third type increases the size of a movement.

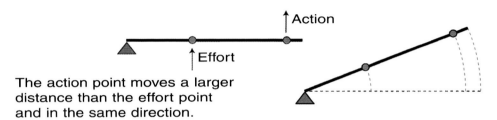

The action point moves a larger distance than the effort point and in the same direction.

USING TYPE 3 LEVERS

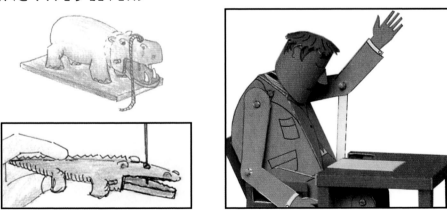

The idea of using a type 3 lever for toys is not a new one as these two examples from ancient Egypt show. The fulcrum in both cases is a hinge that attaches the lower jaw to the head. The effort is provided by pulling the string. In the modern automaton the fulcrum is his shoulder and the representative's hand is raised by a rod at his elbow whenever he is required to vote.

LEVERS OF THE SECOND TYPE:

The effort point and the action point both lie on the same sides of the fulcrum with the effort point further from the fulcrum.

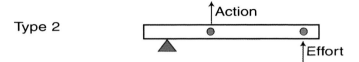

A lever of the second type reduces the size of a movement.

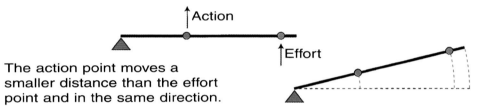

The action point moves a smaller distance than the effort point and in the same direction.

Type 2 levers are not as useful in paper automata as the other two types because they reduce the speed and size of a movement, something that is very seldom required in a design.

FULCRUMS AND HINGES

In order to make all kinds of levers work properly, a good, friction free fulcrum is necessary, one that can work over and over again.

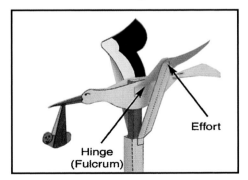

A paper hinge makes a simple yet remarkably effective kind of fulcrum. This stork model has two such fulcrums at the points where the wings join the body. The flapping wings are type 3 levers. Two folded pushrods provide the 'effort' and the effect of the levers is to increase the distance travelled by the tips of the wings. See also page 16.

Fulcrums can also be small pieces of cocktail stick or matches and they can be very unobtrusive. Much more obtrusive but very easy to use are the brass paper fasteners obtainable from stationery shops.

CAMS & CRANKSHAFTS

CAMS

When a circular disc rotates about an axle at its centre, every point remains at the same distance from the axle.

However, if the same disc rotates about a shaft which is not at its centre, then the distance from the axle changes smoothly between a minimum and a maximum. The word 'cam' is used to describe a disc operating in this fashion and cams of various kinds are immensely useful in paper automata design.

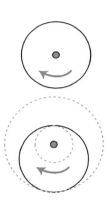

EGG-SHAPED CAMS

If the cam is egg-shaped rather than a perfect circle then the range between the smallest and greatest distances from the shaft can be considerably increased. Such cams, made of a single or double thickness card, are very useful in smoothly raising and lowering a pushrod.

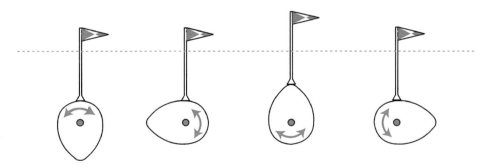

In this diagram the pushrod is represented simply as a pole with a flag on it and the red dotted line serves as a reference to show how the varying distances of the circumference from the axle are transferred elsewhere. The pushrod is kept in contact with the cam solely by the force of gravity.

Because the outline of this cam is essentially a smooth one, the handle can be turned either way. Because the cam is symmetrical, the motion of the flag would be the same in either case.

SNAIL CAMS

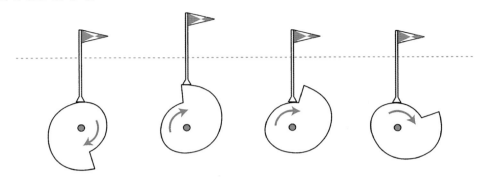

Cams with a snail-like shape like this are very useful for paper engineers. They can provide a discontinuity, a sudden change of shaft distance, so producing a slow rise of the pushrod followed by a sudden drop. However, it is important to realise that snail-cams can only be rotated in one direction, in this case, clockwise. Metal cams in engines, clocks and watches can use springs to keep the pushrod in contact with the cam but in paper models this is not possible. The pushrod can only drop under the influence of gravity and it is therefore important that any sleeves and guides are sufficiently loose.

JAGGED CAMS

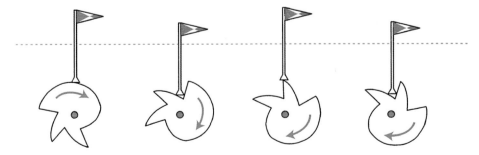

Cams can have several jagged teeth and they will then produce a repeating sequence of rather jerky movements. By adjusting the shapes and positions of the teeth this sequence can be fine-tuned to produce a desired pattern of actions. In fact, designing a perfect shape for a cam to achieve some particular purpose is a fascinating and rewarding activity which offers plenty of scope for creativity.

CAMS & CRANKSHAFTS

MULTIPLE CAMS

If several cams are placed on the same shaft then it is possible to produce several different kinds of motion at the same time.

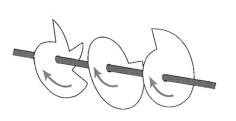

The set of multiple cams which drive this automaton is a particularly fine example of their use. Turning the handle smoothly causes each of the three sheep to hop in a different and rather unsynchronised way. It is the jagged cam which operates the lamb and it hops three times for every once by the adults.

Note how the base of the 'pushrod' in this model is not free-standing but is actually a hinged flap, glued to the framework. The flap follows the outline of the cam and drops decisively whenever it passes the discontinuity. The weight of the rod and the sheep is enough to guarantee a rapid drop and a very energetic and lively motion.

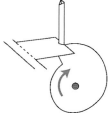

USING CRANKSHAFTS

If a shaft is bent into a U-shape so that it forms a 'crankshaft', then it can be used to transform a smooth circular motion into an oval motion.

The action of a crankshaft does not produce a pure linear motion as a cam and pushrod does but when a rod operated by a crankshaft is passed through a relatively small hole or slot in a framework, the free end then traces out a rather uneven curve in space.

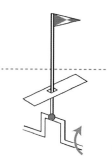

CONNECTING TO A CRANKSHAFT

The hole or 'gate' should be just large enough to allow free movement of the rod. It is evident that a low gate produces a larger movement of the free end and a high gate a smaller one. To obtain the kind of motion needed it is best to experiment with different heights of rod.

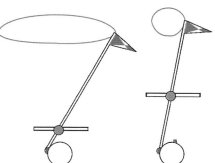

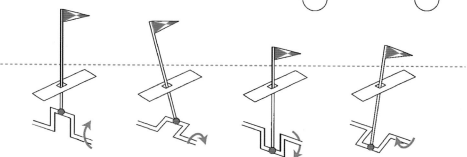

The attachment of the rod to the crankshaft cannot be fixed and so a loose joint is required. A loop of paper or double washer shape is usually all that is needed to provide a satisfactory connection.

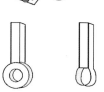

Because the drive rod is attached to the crankshaft in this fashion, this kind of mechanism does not depend on the force of gravity. Nor does the rod need to be vertical in order to transfer power.

DOUBLE CRANKSHAFTS

Crankshafts with two or more U-shapes are often used in real engineering to produce more complicated kinds of motion. However, while working entirely in paper, it is not a good idea to attempt to use a crankshaft which operates more than two separate driver rods.

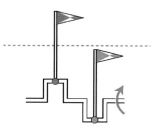

CRANK SLIDERS

CRANK SLIDERS

If a rod operated by a turning crankshaft is passed through a tube which is attached by a hinge to the base rather than passing through a simple gate, then it is called a 'crank slider'.

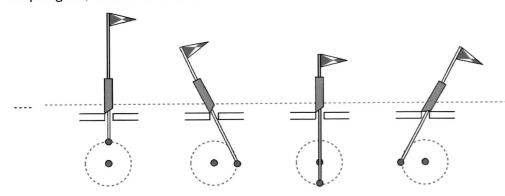

At first sight, it might seem that this arrangement offers no advantage at all over a slot or gate in the frame. After all the flag end follows exactly the same curve as it would if the sleeve were not there.

However, the function and purpose of such sleeves is to carry a semi-fixed surface upwards to a place where it can be used to act in opposition to the movement of the pushrod passing through it.

As we have already seen on page 11, for this automaton the sleeve provides fixed points for the pivots at the base of the wings. The pushrod moves the body up and down, so causing the wings to flap.

Note that the sleeve is glued to the framework by a flap which acts as a hinge. Also note how the base of the sleeve has been cut away so that it can swing back and forth as the crank handle is turned.

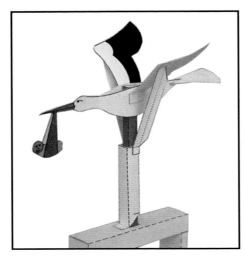

RED DRAGON

Here the crank slider in the form of a kebab stick has been made to operate the jaws of a ferocious-looking dragon.

Notice how the feet are glued to the base and how the geometrical crank slider used for the stork has now been transformed into parts of the body of the dragon. There is sufficient flexibility in the folds of the paper to deal with the three-dimensional motion and to give it a very lively feel. This automaton also uses three lengths of fine string to operate the lower jaws, the forelegs and the wings.

RED KNIGHT

If the back legs of the horse were not fixed to the base, then the knight and his horse would just bob about in the air in a rather uninteresting and unconvincing fashion.

However, the existence of these fixed points and the joints at the tops of the legs permit adjustments to the proportions. By experimenting with these proportions it is possible to fine-tune the motion.

LINKAGES & JOINTS

LINKAGES USING WOODEN JOINTS

In this demonstration model a rod driven by the crankshaft is linked by means of a joint made from a spent match to a lever pivoted at one end. The free end of the lever traces out an arc of a circle.

This automaton, called 'The Weight of Bureaucracy' shows how a succession of levers can be set up to produce a quite complicated sequence of actions. The arm itself is a type 1 lever and is quite heavy. It is pivoted in such a way that its own weight causes it to descend on to the head of the poor unfortunate underneath whenever the operating cam allows it. As it descends, a secondary lever system lowers the worker through the platform, giving the impression that he is being hammered into the ground. In this case the levers are operated by a cam, not a crankshaft. Note that the cam is operating a lever which is underneath, not above as is a more usual technique.

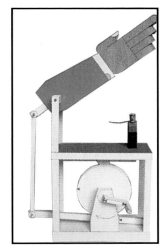

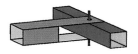 

These diagrams show how two square rods can be jointed using a wooden peg and how a single rod can be pivoted about an end.

JOINTS USING PAPER ONLY

For some paper engineers it is considered a point of principle to construct all parts of an automaton using nothing but paper and glue. Paper joints and hinges can be surprisingly strong and flexible if properly designed and will often operate many hundreds of times without tearing and weakening. Even if they do, a repair with plastic tape will soon give them a new lease of life.

Joints from paper hinges

This rather elegant mechanism for an automaton called 'Busy Buzzy Bees' uses a pair of pushrods at opposite sides to make the bees move in a rather random-seeming and busy way. There are two identical linkages but do note the use of colour to distinguish between what would otherwise be identical parts.

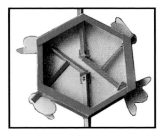

For any automaton that is to be sold as a kit and made up by someone else, this kind of thoughtfulness is essential. The rods are kept in the same plane by means of slots and sliders, a useful paper engineering technique which is explained in the section entitled 'limiting movement' on page 19.

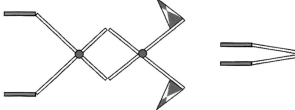 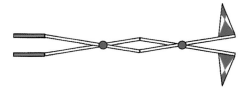

This idea, based on 'lazy-tongs' which some people use to extend their reach, might well form the basis of a linkage mechanism for a paper engineer. It would work best with two wooden joints and four paper hinge joints.

FRICTION DRIVES & GEARWHEELS

FRICTION DRIVE

An important and necessary technique when designing paper automata is to be able to change the speed and direction of a rotary motion. The simplest way, and one which is very effective, is to allow the edge of one circular disc to rub on the under surface of another disc. Using friction transfers a force from one wheel to another, hence the name 'friction drive'. Rather surprisingly there is usually little slipping and even where there is, it does no harm.

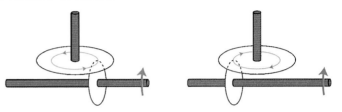

This paper automaton shows a reed bed. The turning handle is connected directly to a vertical wheel which turns a horizontal wheel and causes a collection of ducks to emerge from the shelter of the reeds into open water at the front and then to disappear back inside again. It is a simple mechanism and it is easy to make it work well. All the shafts are made from either cocktail sticks or kebab sticks.

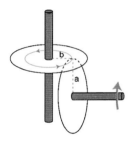

This diagram shows the important features of a friction wheel drive. The circumference of the lower disc is $2\pi a$ and the effective circumference of the upper disc is $2\pi b$. The ratio of the speeds of rotation is in proportion to these circumferences and therefore to their effective radii a and b.

If a is greater than b then the speed of rotation of the upper disc is greater than that of the lower disc. If a is less than b then the speed of rotation of the upper disc is less than that of the lower disc.
For a reliable operation the overall radius of the upper disc should exceed b by 7 or 8 mm.

The two wheels need to be in exact horizontal and vertical planes because it is the force of gravity which keeps them in contact. If the lower disc were not vertical, then its edges would quickly bend and distort and the mechanism would fail.

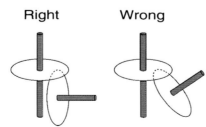

Right   Wrong

REVERSING THE DIRECTION

Assuming that the handle on the lower disc always turns in the same clockwise direction, the upper disc can be made to turn either clockwise or anticlockwise depending on which side of its vertical axis the lower disc makes contact.

The automaton 'Wimbledon' uses this concept in a very elegant way so that heads of the members of the audience turn back and forth in unison as the rally continues.

The secret is to have two driving wheels on the same shaft for each person and then to cut away opposite parts of their circumferences. This means that only one vertical wheel remains in contact with the horizontal wheel at any one time. Observe that by using three separate friction wheels the three spectators could become unsynchronised should there be slippage in one but not the others.

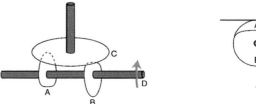

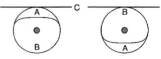

View from D

FRICTION DRIVES & GEARWHEELS

A VARIABLE SPEED DRIVE

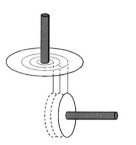

It is easy to make a variable speed friction wheel. It just needs to be possible to push the drive shaft in and out, so increasing and reducing the effective radius of the upper wheel. The closer to the centre of the upper wheel, the greater the speed of rotation.

Remember that the vertical shaft has to be very loosely guided. It is the weight of the upper unit which keeps the two wheels in contact.

PAPER GEARWHEELS

Another way to change the speed and direction of a rotary motion is to use a gearwheel. It also makes possible the introduction of the concept of the ratchet, essential for motion limited to a single direction. While no doubt other paper gearwheel designs are possible, here is a very elegant one because the design automatically doubles the thickness of the paper at just those points where it is most needed.

Construction

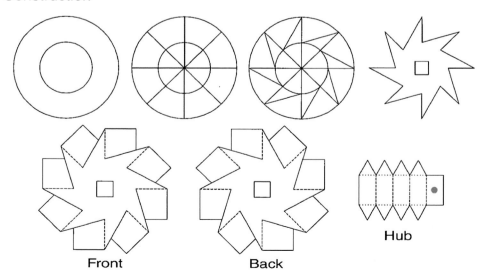

Front   Back   Hub

CHANGING THE SPEED OF ROTATION

Paper gearwheels made exactly to the printed design below left have 8 teeth and all the faces which take the pressure are of double thickness. Although it is theoretically possible to design such gearwheels with any number of teeth, the level of care needed to get a good smooth-running action increases with the number of teeth. Generally it is best to limit yourself to between eight and sixteen.

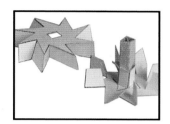

Gearwheels made using this method will mesh together in the same plane and then serve to change the speed of rotation and to reverse its direction. The ratio of the speeds is inversely proportional to the number of teeth. In this example, the wheel with 8 teeth will run 1.5 times faster than the wheel with 12 teeth.

CHANGING THE PLANE OF ROTATION

By setting the shafts of two of these gearwheels at right angles it is possible to change the motion to a different plane.

This working demonstration model shows two meshing gearwheels set at right angles to each other. Each of them has eight teeth and so the speed of rotation of the vertical axle is the same as the speed of the rotation of the handle. The demonstration model 4, called 'Meshing Gearwheels', has 12 teeth on the drive shaft and 8 teeth on the flagstaff ensuring that the flag turns one and a half times for every single turn of the handle.

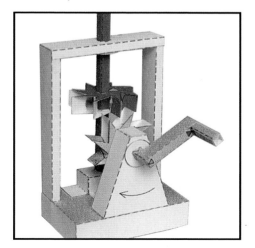

LIMITING MOVEMENT

RATCHETS, PAWLS AND TRIPS

A ratchet is a useful device which allows a motion to take place in one direction only.

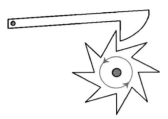

In this mechanism the ratcheting effect is obtained by a carefully shaped pawl which drops into place each time that the gearwheel has moved on by one tooth. It drops solely under the influence of gravity.

In this case the gearwheel can only turn in an anticlockwise direction as the square edge of the pawl prevents any clockwise movement.

This cam is known as a trip-cam because it only engages and trips the gearwheel once each turn of the handle. In fact it behaves like a gearwheel with a single tooth.

The trip-cam turning in a clockwise direction causes the gearwheel to turn in an anticlockwise direction.

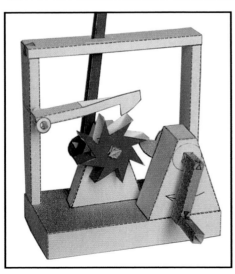

This demonstration model illustrates how a gearwheel, a trip-cam and a pawl can be combined to move a crankshaft one step at a time as the handle is turned.

Without the pawl there is a tendency, due to the flexibility of paper, for the cogwheel not to trip decisively into the next position.

LEVERS AND GUIDED CAMS

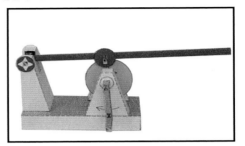

This model shows how a cam operated by a handle can be made to raise and lower a beam within certain limits. It is actually an example of the use of a type 3 lever. Its effect is to magnify the changing radius of the cam so that the free end moves further and more quickly as a consequence. Further levers could be operated from any point on that primary lever. The guides for the cam are in the form of circular disks but of course could be of any shape.

This automaton uses exactly the same principle as the demonstration model illustrated above. Here, the square type 3 lever is indeed used to push a secondary rod upwards to reproduce the motion of a small boat on a moderately choppy sea. It is the shaped cam which ultimately limits and controls the motion of this pushrod and thus the boat. The cam runs in a guide glued to both sides of the primary lever.

LIMITING MOVEMENT

DESIGNING THE GUIDES

This model uses a cam to control a rather complex arrangement.

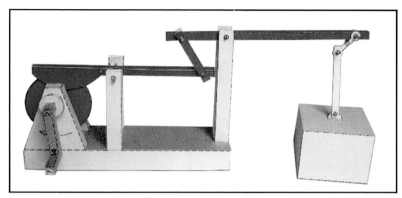

However, it is more a demonstration model than an automaton because it does not do anything especially exciting. All that happens is that the block lifts up off the ground and then puts itself down again! It has been included because it is a very nice example of paper engineering and shows how levers can operate levers and how a cam operating a cam follower can control it all.

It also demonstrates a valuable technique to use whenever a cam operates a cam follower, whatever its shape. The technique is to make a pair of identical cams and to place them side by side on the same shaft, separated by two or three millimetres. This produces a more stable and stronger arrangement than simply doubling the thickness of a single cam.

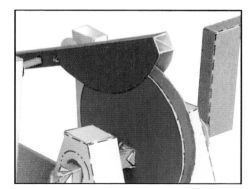

To avoid the cam sticking on surplus glue or jamming in a crack, it is always best to insert an additional U-shaped guide between the visible guides on the cam follower.

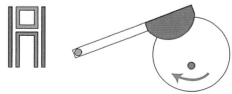

LUGS AND PINS

Here are two further ways in which a cam, in this case a snail-cam, can be made to cause a lever to rise and fall in an uneven but controlled fashion. In both cases the handle can only be turned in a clockwise direction. Note also the use of double cams to give a more stable mechanism. Because of the flexibility of paper, both the lug and the pin should be made appreciably longer that the total width of the cams.

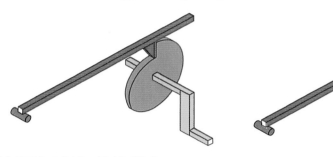

SLOTS AND SLIDERS

This automaton has six bees which move about in an interesting and rather confusing way when the opposing pushrods are operated. Four of the bees are glued to H-shaped sliders which move in slots, two straight and two curved. The other two bees twist in an irregular way and add to the air of activity. For a picture of the linkages see page 15.

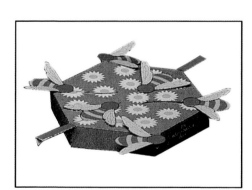

To avoid the H-shaped slider catching on the sides of the slot, it is best to create the H from two U-shaped guides glued back to back. An additional strengthening layer top and bottom can be added if required.

POWER SOURCES

TURNING HANDLES

The demonstration models in this book all rely on the power provided by turning a handle on a shaft. That shaft can then operate a cam or it can be formed into a crankshaft.

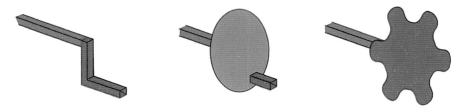

The first handle is the familiar one, the second shows how a length of square shaft can be let into a circular disc and the third one shows how a circular disc can be cut to provide finger holds. This third one also looks a more interesting shape and gives a more sophisticated appearance to the finished model.

SIMPLE LEVER HANDLES

It is possible to make automata work by asking the operator either to operate a straight handle for the motley man or to press on a lever in the case of the pecking hen. This first mechanism is reminiscent of those used for one-armed bandits in an amusement arcade. When the handle is operated he bows stiffly like a man with a bad back!

STRING POWER

In cases where the force only pulls and never pushes then it may be a good idea to consider using a string or a cord.

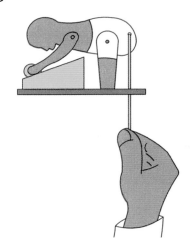

Simple as this model appears to be, it is a very satisfying and pleasing example of the designer's art. It has a fixed leg and a moveable arm and as soon as the pressure is taken off the string, then the force of gravity returns it to the position shown. When the string is pulled, the body becomes more upright. The pivot at the shoulder allows the roller to remain in contact with the surface. It therefore gives the impression of someone rolling out pasta or pastry.

GRAVITY POWER

Another interesting and imaginative use of the force of gravity to power an automaton lies in designing models which will walk independently down a gentle slope. Such 'walking automata' require a lot of care to get the centre of gravity in just the right place relative to the fixed and moving feet, but when everything is just right they will descend the slope with an interesting rocking gait and a satisfactory clicking noise.

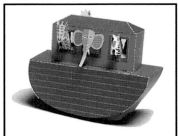

These two walking automata were suggested by the blue-footed boobies found on the Galapagos Islands and the story of Noah's Ark where the animals went aboard two by two.

POWER SOURCES

SAND POWER

The idea of fine sand falling through a narrow aperture is used in the classic egg-timer. They are made symmetrical and so can be used either way up. However, the power stored in the sand is not used. The property that is used is solely that dry sand falling through a narrow aperture always takes the same time to do so. With the right amount of sand they are used as egg timers.

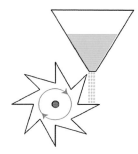

The energy of falling sand can also be used to power paper automata, with the added advantage that they seem to move without human intervention. The best sand for this purpose is that used for bird cages. It may be necessary to sieve out pieces of lime or bone first!

Of course the sand has to be replaced in the hopper and how to achieve that is an important part of the designing process.

THE PIANIST

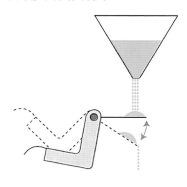

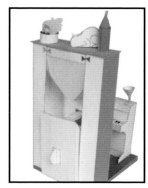

The sand drops from its reservoir on to a pivoted horizontal lever and causes it to descend and the arms to rise. When the sand slides off the sloping lever, it rises and the arms descend. This continues until the hopper is empty. In this model the sand falls into a removable tray at the bottom which has to be taken out and used to recharge the hopper at the top. It is best to have a spare tray. If not, the sand starts to fall through before the tray is replaced and you get sand everywhere.

THE GYMNAST

The wheel is made of eight triangular hoppers and as the sand falls into one of them its weight causes the wheel to turn randomly clockwise or anticlockwise. It turns and the sand spills out and another hopper begins to fill. As the wheel turns in this irregular way the gymnast swings back and forth on the horizontal bars.

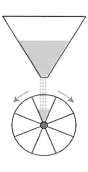

The design is a closed one. To recharge it you have to turn it on one side, then upside down, then on the other side and then upright again.

WATER POWER

While it might seem ridiculous to consider water power for paper models it is well to realise that waterproof paper does exist and may be brought into service for a paper automaton. Consider for instance the paper vases which will hold water for weeks and the books of cut-out and glue paper boats which are available in certain bookshops.

AIR POWER

It is possible to make paper bellows and to use them to pump air but it is hard to make them really airtight. A simple method is to use a paper straw to direct a flow of air to where it is needed. A serious problem is that breath is warm and damp and will soon spoil a paper mechanism. If you want to experiment, try covering the most threatened surfaces with plastic tape.

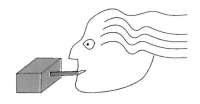

MODELLING

SETTING THE SCENE

Side by side with creating a suitable mechanical movement, paper automata need also to look convincing to the observer. On these pages we concentrate on a variety of paper modelling techniques that help to add interest and relevance to the chosen theme.

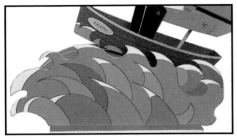  

Flat paper shapes can be cut out with a suitable profile, decorated and then laid down in several layers. Shown here are a stormy sea, a collection of waterside plants and even the flaming entrance to Hell!

MAKING OBJECTS

Convincing objects can be made very simply indeed. For instance, the shadoof bucket is just a cone, and the kite no more than a shaped piece of decorated paper.

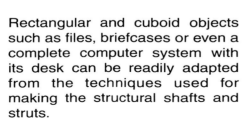

Rectangular and cuboid objects such as files, briefcases or even a complete computer system with its desk can be readily adapted from the techniques used for making the structural shafts and struts.

MAKING LARGER OBJECTS

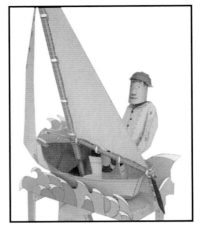 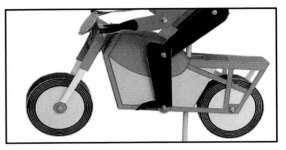

Models of manufactured items require quite a lot of thought and care but can still be built up from simple elements. It is good practice to start by looking at how they are made in reality.

MAKING TREES AND PLANTS

These examples show how different types of plant can be created in a very simple way. Each is perfectly adequate for its situation.

ADDING DETAIL

The addition of simple detail can add a lot to a design.

MODELLING

CREATING CONVINCING BODY SHAPES

Although the bodies of these four characters are all made out of the same basic box shape, they are clearly differentiated by changing the profiles and the proportions.

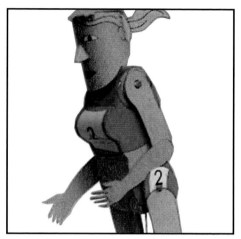

The most obvious differences in these four examples are between the male and the female shapes. However the two men also differ from each other significantly, the rather overweight office-bound politician contrasting with the slim relaxed sailor on his boat.

ADDING CLOTHES AND OTHER ACCESSORIES

Convincing clothes and accessories can make a big difference to the appearance of automata. These two are rather elaborate examples but they do clearly demonstrate how quite complex models can be created from a number of simpler components.

MAKING JOINTED LIMBS

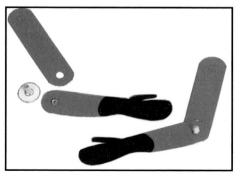

Small pieces of cocktail stick or spent matches can be used to make unobtrusive joints for both people and animals. If unobtrusiveness is not an issue, then plastic poppers or even brass paper fasteners can be used instead.

However, don't forget the effectiveness of simple hinge joints made from a scored paper fold.

MODELLING

MAKING HEADS AND FACES

It is very common for paper automata to include people and so it is necessary to develop a certain skill in creating convincing head and face shapes. Just as good cartoonists are able to evoke the character of their victims in just a few lines, so good automata designers can create the form of a person or an anthropomorphic animal with a minimum of fuss and paper engineering. Some designers use simple cube and box-like forms to represent heads and bodies, whereas others prefer to take a more sculptural approach.

One thing in this field that is very useful is that once a suitable form has been created then it is not difficult to introduce variations which can be called the 'relatives' of the original.

Here are some 'relatives' of the 'Off Road' motorcyclist, all based on a cylinder of paper. Note that in each case the nose is glued on as a separate piece.

VARIATIONS ON A THEME

It just needed a slight variation on the same basic head-shape to create the moving heads for the 'Wimbledon' automaton.

Note how the hats and hair have been made so different from each other and how the same body-shape has been painted differently to produce three quite distinct sets of clothes for the spectators.

While hats and goggles are an easy way to differentiate between different characters, it is also not at all difficult to create very varied hair-styles.

These two figures have a very definite 'Egyptian' feel to them. Note how the white eyes in a darker face suggest the kinds of images seen in Egyptian hieroglyphs and wall paintings.

Teeth are not often an important feature in humans but for animals the modelling of teeth can add dramatically to the impact. Monsters of various kinds make good subjects for automata.

THE FOURTEEN WORKING MECHANISMS

1. CRANK SLIDER

General Instructions:

——————— continuous out-line: cut

- - - - - - - score and bend parts back (hill fold)

············· score and bend parts forwards (valley fold)

—··—··— glue part

● glue (red dot)

⊠ cut out (red cross)

⊠ cut cross (black cross)

Base

- glue tabs

cut out slots

1

Base Support

- glue to underside of base beneath crank support

2

1

Crank Support

- assemble and glue onto base

3d

3c

3a-d

3b

3a

1

Supports

- assemble supports 4a + 4b
- push supports up through base 1 from below and glue

- glue part 4c onto supports

4c

4b

4a

Handle

triangles of same colour must point towards each other

red triangles

5a

5b

5c

Crank Shaft

blue triangles

6a

6b

Crank

7a

7b

Mechanism (rear view)

lever 8

1. form loop with white strip

2. glue blue strip around

make loop and push onto crank

9a+b

glue disks

Final Assembly

- glue flag 10

Operation

When you turn the crank clockwise, the flag will move to and fro and up and down.

The rotation of the crank is converted in an elliptical movement of the flag by the crank slider.

2. OSCILLATING LEVER

General Instructions:

——— continuous out-line: cut

-------- score and bend parts back (hill fold)

············· score and bend parts forwards (valley fold)

—·—·— glue part

● glue (red dot)

⊠ cut out (red cross)

⊠ cut cross (black cross)

Base

- glue tabs

1

Base Support

- glue to underside of base beneath crank support

2

1

Crank Support

- assemble and glue onto base

3b   3c   4

3a

3a-c

Handle

triangles of same colour must point towards each other

red triangles

5a   5b   5c

Crank Shaft

blue triangles

6a

6b

white triangles

7a   7b

Mechanism (side view)

6a   6b   3a-c

5b   7a

5a

1

7b

Final Assembly

8a

9a

8b

9b

8a   11   8a

9b   9a

4   8b

10a+b

1. Insert lever 8a into lever bearing 4 with pin 8b (movable !)
2. Push tie rod 9a onto crankpin 7b and connect lever 8a with pin 9b
3. Glue discs 10a+b und flag 11

Function Test

When you turn the handle clockwise the lever will swing from side to side.
The rotation of the crank shaft is transformed into a pendulum motion.

26

3. FRICTION TRANSFER

———————— continuous out-line: cut

– – – – score and bend parts back (hill fold)

· · · · · · score and bend parts forwards (valley fold)

— · · — glue part

● glue (red dot)

⊠ cut out (red cross)

⊠ cut cross (black cross)

Base

- glue tabs

cut out

1

Base Support

- glue to underside of base beneath crank support

1   2

Crank Support and Shaft Bearing

- assemble and glue on base

3b   3c
3a

4   3a-c
1

Support

- assemble supports 5a + 5b
- push supports up through base 1 from below and glue
- glue part 5c onto supports

5c
5b
5a

Handle

triangles of same colour must point towards each other

red triangles

6a
6b
6c

Crank Shaft

7a
blue triangles
7b

Friction Wheels and Shafts

bend tabs   cut opening

8b

- bend, glue and cut out

9a
9b

- exactly the same: 10a+b and 11a+b

8a
8b
8c

Final Assembly

- push crank shaft into crank support
- push wheel 9, 10 or 11 onto crank shaft (don't glue)
- push output shaft 8a through the opening in part 5c from below and put the lower end in bearing 4
- glue flag 8d

Function Test

When you turn the handle clockwise, the red driven wheel 8b will turn anti-clockwise.

You can push the three driving wheels one after another on the shaft:
The greater the perimeter of the driving wheel, the quicker the driven wheel will rotate.

8d
5c
8a

---

4. MESHING GEARWHEELS

General Instructions:

——— continuous out-line: cut

– – – – score and bend parts back (hill fold)

· · · · · · score and bend parts forwards (valley fold)

— · · — glue part

● glue (red dot)

⊠ cut out (red cross)

⊠ cut cross (black cross)

Base
- glue tabs

cut out

1

Base Support
- glue to underside of base beneath crank support

2

1

Crank Support and Shaft Bearing
- assemble and glue on base

3b   3c

3a

4

3a-c

1

Support
- assemble supports 5a + 5b and push it up through base 1 from below and glue
- glue part 5c onto supports, white triangles point to each other

triangles

5c

5b

5a

Handle
triangles of same colour must point towards each other

red triangles

6a

6b

6c

Crank Shaft
blue triangles

7a

7b

Gearwheels
1. - glue hub 8a onto part 8b
2. - for assembly push part 8c and hub with part 8b onto crank shaft (don't glue !), then glue part 8c to hub
3. - bend tooth flanks and glue to each other
4. - remove gearwheel from crank shaft

① 8b   8a

outside: colour

inside: white

② 8c   7a

③ 8b

tooth flanks   8c

assemble gearwheel 9a-c in the same way

Final Assembly
- assemble output shaft 10a and push from above through the opening in the support
- push washer 10b and gearwheel 8a-c on the shaft from below
- push crank shaft 7a into crank support, then push discs 11 and gearwheel 9a-c

Function Test
- glue both gearwheels when they turn smoothly, otherwise move the driven wheel a little bit
- glue flag 12

The driving wheel has twice as much teeth than the driven wheel, therefore we have a transmission acceleration.

12

10b   8a-c

11

9a-c

5. RATCHET

General Instructions:

——————— continuous out-line: cut

- - - - - - - score and bend parts back (hill fold)

··········· score and bend parts forwards (valley fold)

—··—··— glue part

● glue (red dot)

⊠ cut out (red cross)

⊠ cut cross (black cross)

Base

- glue tabs

cut out slots

1

Base Support

- glue to underside of base beneath shaft suppports

1 2

Crank Support

- assemble and glue on base

3b 3c 4a-c 3a-c

3a 1

Handle

triangles of same colour must point towards each other

red triangles

5a 5b 5c

Crank Shaft

blue triangles

6a 6b

Mechanism (rear view)

- glue three parts of pawl 7a-c,
- push pawl on crank shaft and glue,
- glue part 7d

7a-c 7d

Wheel Shaft

white triangles

8a 8c 8b

Gearwheel

1. - glue hub 9a onto part 9b
2. - for assembly push hub with 9b onto ratchet shaft (but don't glue !), then glue part 9c to the hub
3. - bend tooth flanks and glue to each other
4. - remove gearwheel from shaft

1. 9b 9a

colour is outside

inside: white

2. 9c

3. 8a

tooth flanks

5. RATCHET (CONTINUED)

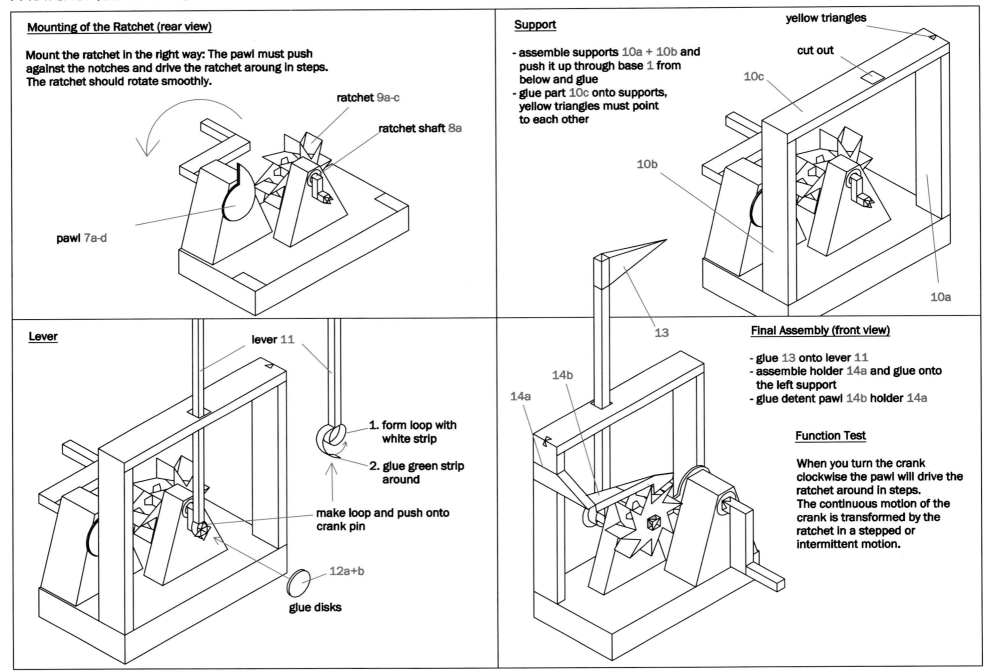

Mounting of the Ratchet (rear view)

Mount the ratchet in the right way: The pawl must push against the notches and drive the ratchet aroung in steps. The ratchet should rotate smoothly.

ratchet 9a-c

ratchet shaft 8a

pawl 7a-d

Support

- assemble supports 10a + 10b and push it up through base 1 from below and glue
- glue part 10c onto supports, yellow triangles must point to each other

yellow triangles

cut out

10c

10b

10a

Lever

lever 11

1. form loop with white strip
2. glue green strip around

make loop and push onto crank pin

12a+b

glue disks

13

14b

14a

Final Assembly (front view)

- glue 13 onto lever 11
- assemble holder 14a and glue onto the left support
- glue detent pawl 14b holder 14a

Function Test

When you turn the crank clockwise the pawl will drive the ratchet around in steps.
The continuous motion of the crank is transformed by the ratchet in a stepped or intermittent motion.

6. Cams & Friction Wheel

General Instructions:

—————— continuous out-line: cut

– – – – score and bend parts back (hill fold)

· · · · · · score and bend parts forwards (valley fold)

— · — glue part

● glue (red dot)

⊠ cut out (red cross)

⊠ cut cross (black cross)

Base

- glue tabs

cut out openings

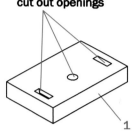

1

Base Support

- glue to underside of base beneath crank support

2

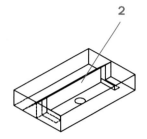

Support

- assemble supports 3a + 3b and push them up through base 1 from below and glue

3c

3b

3a

yellow triangles

white triangles

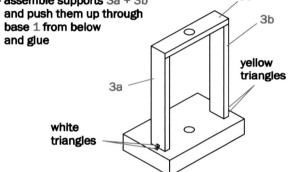

Crank Supports and Stops

- glue

4b   4c

4a

5a-c

6+7

4a-c

6

7

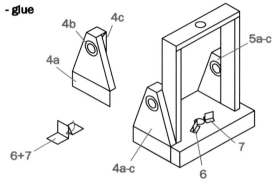

Handle

triangles of same colour must point towards each other

red triangles

8c

8a

8b

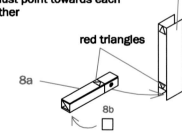

Crank Shaft

blue triangles

9a

9b

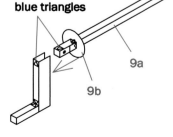

Cam Shaft

- push cam shaft 9a through right crank support (with arrow) and push the staggered (!)cams 10a+b und 11a+b
- glue cam 10a+b back to back and then glue it on the shaft
- as well assemble cam 11a+b and glue it to the shaft
- glue washer 9c

11a+b

10a+b

9c

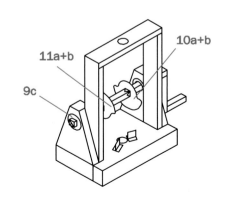

Output Shaft

- assemble output shaft 12a and glue stop 12b+c
- glue friction wheel 13a+b and glue on stiffener 13c
- push friction wheel with stiffener on output shaft and glue

12a

13c

13a

13b

12c+b

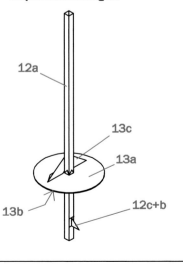

Final Assembly

- put output shaft into the support
- push washer 14 from below and glue
- glue flag 15

Function Test

Turn the handle, and the two cams will swing the friction wheel and the flag back and forth.

15

14

7. Cam & Pushrod

———— continuous out-line: cut

- - - - - - score and bend parts back (hill fold)

· · · · · · · · · score and bend parts forwards (valley fold)

— · — · — glue part

⊠ cut out (red cross)

● glue (red dot)

Base

- glue tabs

cut out slots

1

Base Support

- glue underside of base beneath crank support

2

1

Crank Support

- assemble and glue on base

3b

3c

4a-c

3a-c

3a

1

Handle

triangles of same colour must point towards each other

red triangles

5a

5b

5c

Crank Shaft

blue triangles

6a

6b

Support

- glue guiding 7a+b
- glue supports 7c+d

7b

7d

7a

7c

Final Assembly

- push supports 7c+d into base and glue
- push pushrod 8a with flag 8b through guiding and glue discs 8c+d at the bottom
- glue tubes 9b+c onto excentric disc 9a
- hold excentric disc between both crank supports and insert crank shaft

9b

9c

9a

In the same way as the excentric disc you can assemble the snail cam 10a-c, the egg shaped cam 11a-c and the disc cam 12a-c and insert them into the model and test.

Attention: The snail cam only works in one sense of rotation!

8b

8a

8c+d

8. CAM & LEVER

General Instructions:

————	continuous out-line: cut
– – – –	score and bend parts back (hill fold)
· · · · · ·	score and bend parts forwards (valley fold)
— · · —	glue part
●	glue (red dot)

⊠ cut out (red cross)
⊠ cut cross (black cross)

Base

- glue tabs

1

Base Support

- glue to underside of base beneath crank support

2

Crank Support and Axle Bearing

- assemble crank support 3a-c and 4a-c and axle bearing 5 and glue on base

4a-c
5
3a-c
3b
3c
3a

Handle

triangles of same colour must point towards each other

red triangles

6a
6b
6c

Crank Shaft

blue triangles

7a
7b

Lever and Pin

- glue pin 8b on lever 8a
- glue guiding disc 8c on pin

8a
8b
8c

Axle

- push axle 9a in bearing 5
- glue washers 9b and 9c
- glue lever 8a

9a
9b
9c
8a

Flag

- glue flag 10 to lever 8a

Cams

- double strength of cam 11a by bending
- glue tubes 11b and 11c
- assemble cams 12a-c, 13a-c and 14a-c
- push the cams on the shaft and test the movement of the lever (don't glue)

Three cams only work in one sense of rotation!

11a
11b
11c

General View

10
13a-c

9. Happy Birthday

General Instructions:

_____ continuous out-line: cut

-------- score and bend parts back (hill fold)

············ score and bend parts forwards (valley fold)

—·—··— glue part

● glue (red dot)

⊠ cut out (red cross)

⊠ cut cross (black cross)

Base

- glue tabs

cut out slots

1

Base Support

- glue to underside of base beneath crank support

2

1

Crank Support

- assemble and glue onto base

3c

3d

3a-d

3b   3a

1

Supports

- assemble supports 4a + 4b
- push supports up through base 1 from below and glue
- glue part 4c onto supports

cut out

4b

4c

4a

Handle

triangles of same colour must point towards each other

red triangles

5a

5b

5c

Crank Shaft

blue triangles

6a

6b

Crank

7a

7b

Mechanism (rear view)

lever 8

1. form loop with white strip

2. glue yellow strip around

make loop and push onto crank

9a+b

glue disks

Final Assembly

- glue tube 10
- glue stork 11a to lever 8
- glue tail 11b
- glue wings 11c + d
- glue tie rods 12a + b to tube and wings

If you want you can glue more babies to the stork's beak.

11d   11b

11a

11c

12a

10

Function Test

When you turn the handle clockwise, the stork moves up and down and to and fro.

10. At the Duck's Pond

──────── continuous out-line: cut

-------- score and bend parts back (hill fold)

············ score and bend parts forwards (valley fold)

─·─·─ glue part

● glue (red dot)

⊠ cut out (red cross)

⊠ cut cross (black cross)

Box Base / Box Top

- glue tabs

2

1

cut out

Base Support

- glue to underside of base beneath crank support

3

1

Crank Support and Shaft Bearing

- assemble and glue on base

cut out

5

4b

4c

4a

4a-c

Handle

triangles of same colour must point towards each other

red triangles

6a

6b

6c

Crank Shaft

blue triangles

7a

7b

1.

8b

colour is outside

inside: white

8a

Driving Wheel

1. - glue hub 8a onto part 8b
2. - for assembly push part 8c and hub with part 8b onto the crank shaft (don't glue!), then glue part 8c to hub
3. - bend tooth flanks and glue to each other
4. - remove the gearwheel from the crank shaft

2.

8c

7a

3.

8b

8c

tooth flanks

Output Shaft

- assemble output shaft 9
- assemble driven gearwheel 10a-c like the driving wheel 8a-c
- push gearwheel and washer 11 on the shaft and glue

Mechanism (view from the left)

8a-c

4a-c

7b

green triangles

7a

1

11

yellow triangles

10a-c

9

35

Box

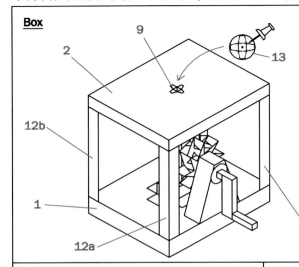

- assemble supports 12a-d
- push supports up through base 1 from below and glue
- put the complete output shaft 9 (including 10a-c and 11) into bearing 5 on the base
- glue box top 2 on supports, push output shaft through the opening in the box top and bend the tabs
- push a needle through the centre of connecting disc 13, glue disc on tabs of output shaft. This small hole made by the needle is important to center the rotating disk with ducks later on.

Rotating Disk

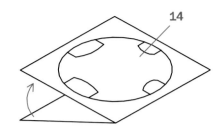

- bend white area and glue on back of the rotating disk 14
- cut out

Ducks

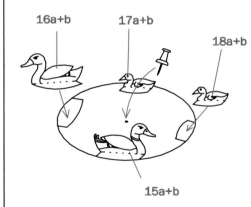

- glue together both sides of the ducks and then glue onto the rotating disk
- push a needle through the dot in the middle of the disk

Glue Rotating Disk

- find the centre of the connecting disk 13 by the help of the needle, then glue the rotating disk 14
- remove the needle

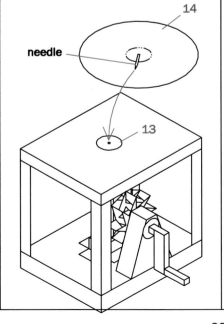

Reed

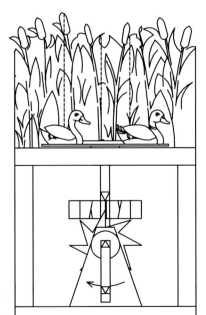

- glue reed 19a on the back of the box
- bend reed 19b and glue onto the box top and the tabs of reed 19a
- bend 19b, so that the ducks can swim smoothly through the openings in the reed
- glue the waterlilies 20a+b und 21a+b as you want

Function Test

When you turn the handle clockwise, then the rotating disk with the ducks will rotate anti-clockwise.

The speed of both gearwheels is the same, as both wheels have the same number of teeth.

11. Pyramid Lifter

——————— continuous out-line: cut

-------- score and bend parts back (hill fold)

·············· score and bend parts forwards (valley fold)

—·—··— glue part

● glue (red dot)

⊠ cut out (red cross)

⊠ cut cross (black cross)

Box Base/Box Top

- cut out openings
- glue tabs
- glue box top 2 onto 1

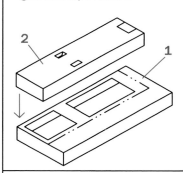

Base Support

- glue to underside

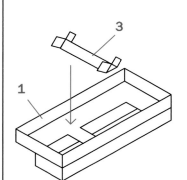

Support

- assemble bearing of right lever 4a-e and glue in box top 2 (white triangles on 4a and 4c must point towards each other)
- assemble bearing of left lever 5a and 5b and glue in box top
- glue connecting part 5c
- glue connecting part 6
- glue connecting part 7
- assemble crank supports 8a-c and 9a-c and glue

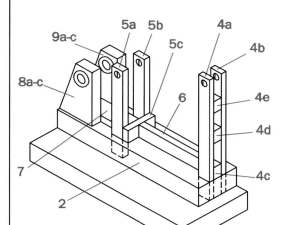

Handle

triangles of same colour must point towards each other

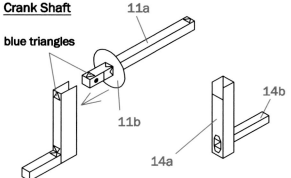

red triangles

Crank Shaft

blue triangles

Excentric Disc

- glue 12b onto 12a
- push 12c and 12a (including 12b) on crank shaft 11a (for assembling)
- glue 12c to 12b
- remove excentric disc from crank shaft

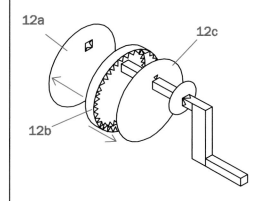

Assembling of the Mechanism (view from the right)

- push crank shaft 11a through crank support 9a from behind
- push excentric disc 12a-c on crank shaft and glue (yellow triangles)
- push crank shaft through second support 8a
- glue crank 14a (with 14b) to crank shaft

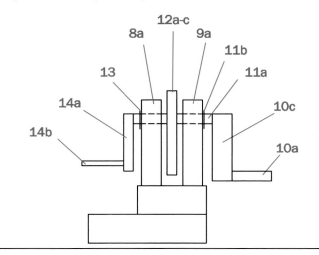

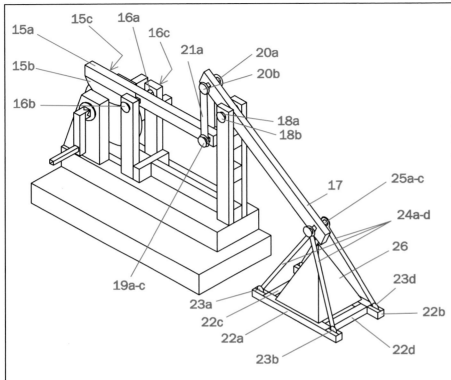

Levers and Pyramid

- assemble lever 15a, glue guidings 15b and 15c and put it into the left bearing with axle 16a
- assemble lever 17 and put it in the right bearing with axle 18a
- install pin 19a and 20a
- push linkages 21a and 21b on pins 19a and 20a and connect both levers in that way
- assemble frame 22a - 22d
- glue loops 23a - 23d onto frame
- cut out linkages 24a - 24d
- roll 25a to make a tube and push into the hole in lever 17, then put in 24a - 24d and glue discs 25b and 25c, glue the bottom ends to loops 23a- 23d
- assemble the pyramid 26 and glue onto the frame

Function Test

Turn the handle 10 clockwise (arrow!): The levers lift and lower and so they lift and lower the pyramid.

Troubleshooting

If the pyramid really lifts but doesn't lower, then presumably the axles 16 and 18 are jamming. Proposal: Take off both axles and smooth out and widen both axle bearings by turning a pencil in the holes. If necessary glue weight (a coin) under the pyramid. When the mechanism works well, then glue discs 16b+c, 18b+c, 19b+c and 20b+c onto axles and pins.

Trunk and Arms

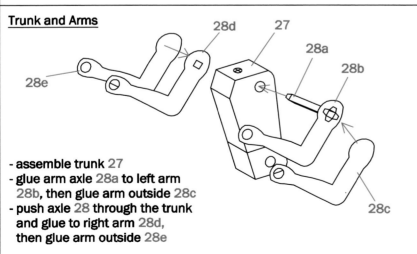

- assemble trunk 27
- glue arm axle 28a to left arm 28b, then glue arm outside 28c
- push axle 28 through the trunk and glue to right arm 28d, then glue arm outside 28e

Legs and Body

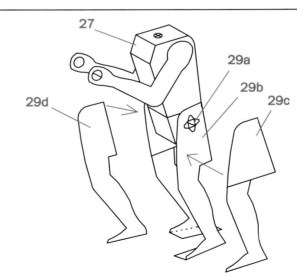

- put trunk 27 to legs 29b with leg axle 29a (movable)
- glue leg outsides 29c and 29d

Head

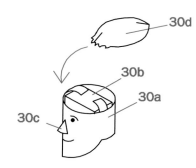

30d
30b
30a
30c

Neck

roll neck with help of a toothpick and glue, remove stick

30e

it is useful to cut the neck tube 30e pointed, so you can turn it into head and body much easier

Final Assembly

- glue head to body
- glue figure to box base, push hands on crank pin 14b
- glue disc 31 to crank pin

Function Test

When you turn the handle clockwise, the excentric disc will lift the first lever and this will lift the second lever bearing the pyramide. The Egyptian worker will move his trunk and arms and it seems as if he would move the device.

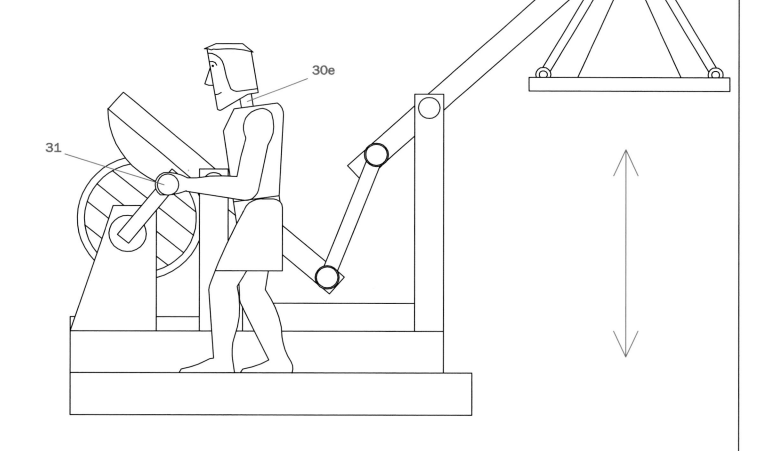

30e

31

12. The Weight of Bureaucracy

General Instructions:

——— continuous out-line: cut

– – – – score and bend parts back (hill fold)

······· score and bend parts forwards (valley fold)

— · — glue part

● glue (red dot)

○ ⊠ cut out (red cross)

⊕ ⊠ cut cross (black cross)

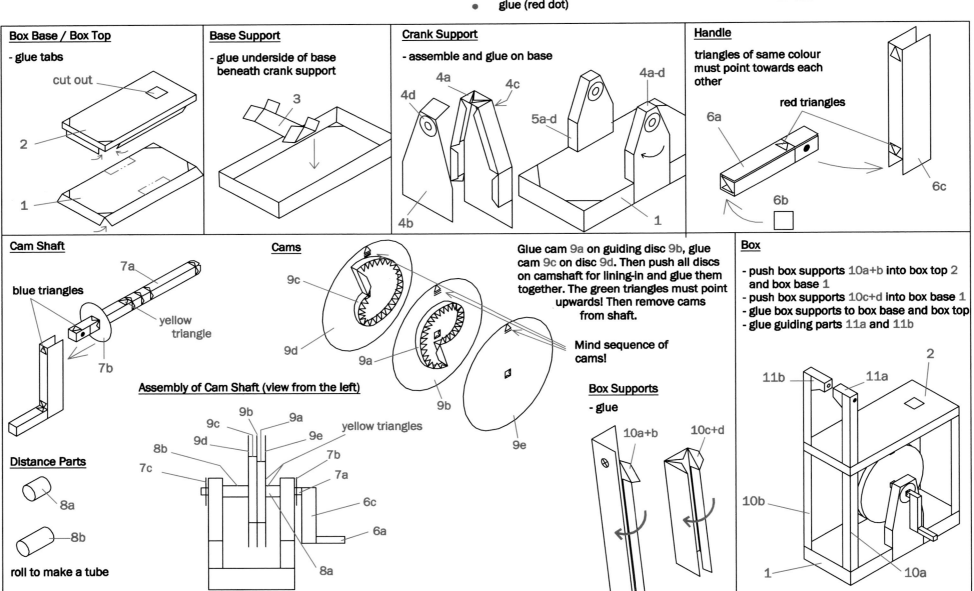

Box Base / Box Top
- glue tabs

cut out

2

1

Base Support
- glue underside of base beneath crank support

3

Crank Support
- assemble and glue on base

4a
4c
4d
4b
5a-d
4a-d
1

Handle

triangles of same colour must point towards each other

red triangles

6a
6b
6c

Cam Shaft

blue triangles

7a
7b
yellow triangle

Distance Parts

8a
8b

roll to make a tube

Cams

9c
9d
9a
9b
9e

Glue cam 9a on guiding disc 9b, glue cam 9c on disc 9d. Then push all discs on camshaft for lining-in and glue them together. The green triangles must point upwards! Then remove cams from shaft.

Mind sequence of cams!

Assembly of Cam Shaft (view from the left)

9b
9c
9a
9d
9e
8b
7c
7b
7a
6c
6a
8a
yellow triangles

Box Supports
- glue

10a+b
10c+d

Box

- push box supports 10a+b into box top 2 and box base 1
- push box supports 10c+d into box base 1
- glue box supports to box base and box top
- glue guiding parts 11a and 11b

11b
11a
2
10b
10a
1

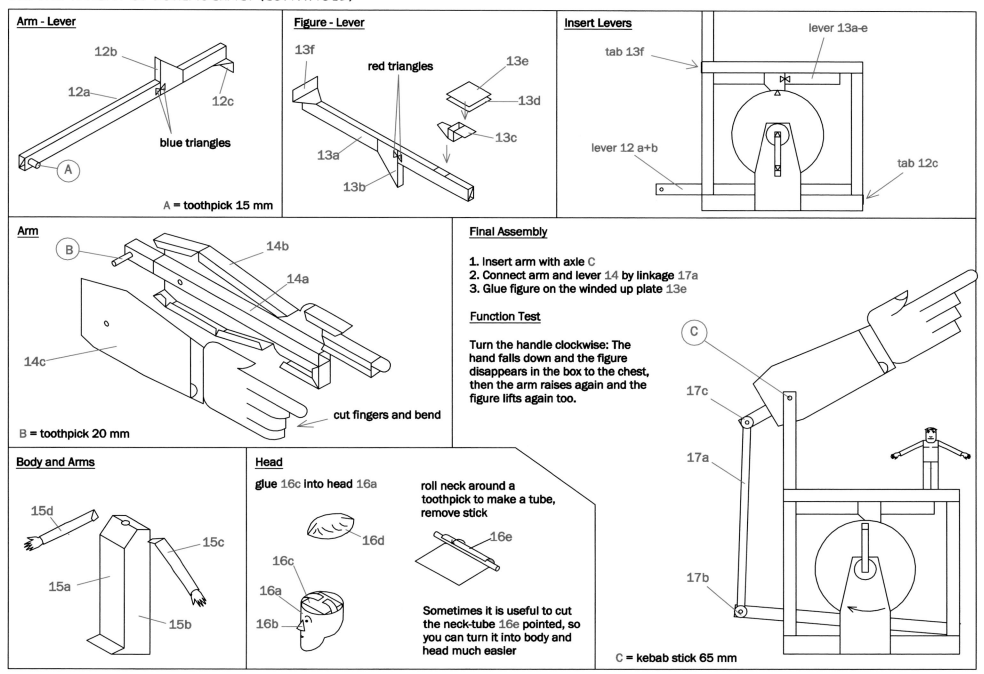

Arm - Lever

12b
12a
12c
blue triangles
A
A = toothpick 15 mm

Figure - Lever

13f
red triangles
13e
13d
13c
13a
13b

Insert Levers

lever 13a-e
tab 13f
lever 12 a+b
tab 12c

Arm

B
14b
14a
14c
B = toothpick 20 mm
cut fingers and bend

Final Assembly

1. Insert arm with axle C
2. Connect arm and lever 14 by linkage 17a
3. Glue figure on the winded up plate 13e

Function Test

Turn the handle clockwise: The hand falls down and the figure disappears in the box to the chest, then the arm raises again and the figure lifts again too.

C
17c
17a
17b
C = kebab stick 65 mm

Body and Arms

15d
15c
15a
15b

Head

glue 16c into head 16a

roll neck around a toothpick to make a tube, remove stick

16d
16e
16c
16a
16b

Sometimes it is useful to cut the neck-tube 16e pointed, so you can turn it into body and head much easier

13. PIANIST

General Instructions:

——— continuous out-line: cut

-------- score and bend parts back (hill fold)

············ score and bend parts forwards (valley fold)

—·—··— glue part

● glue (red dot)

⊠ cut out (red cross)

⊕ cut cross (black cross)

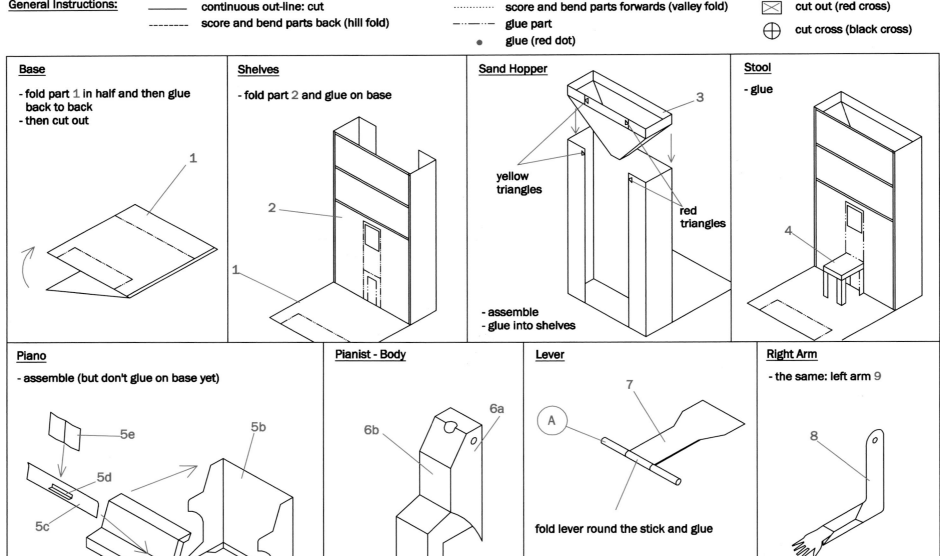

Base

- fold part 1 in half and then glue back to back
- then cut out

1

Shelves

- fold part 2 and glue on base

2

1

Sand Hopper

3

yellow triangles

red triangles

- assemble
- glue into shelves

Stool

- glue

4

Piano

- assemble (but don't glue on base yet)

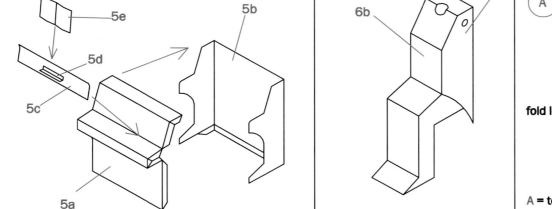

5e

5d

5c

5a

5b

Pianist - Body

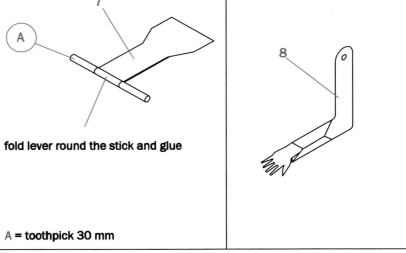

6a

6b

Lever

7

A

fold lever round the stick and glue

A = toothpick 30 mm

Right Arm

- the same: left arm 9

8

Mechanism

- bend fingers down
- insert axle A with lever 7 into the figure
- glue arms
- put figure on stool to try out (don't glue yet)
- hands must lie on the piano's keys
- make lever horizontal

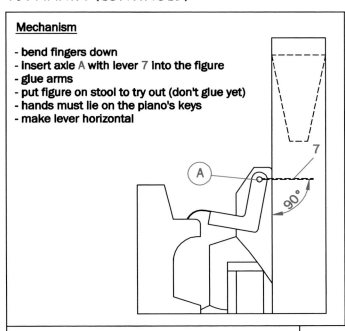

Head

glue head support 10b into head 10a

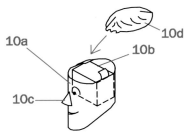

Neck

roll neck round a toothpick to make a tube, glue, remove stick

- glue head on neck
- don't glue neck too deep into body, it shouldn't block lever's axle
Then:
- glue pianist on stool
- glue piano on base

Sometimes it is useful to cut the neck tube pointed, so you can turn it into body and head much easier.

Cover of the Sand Hopper

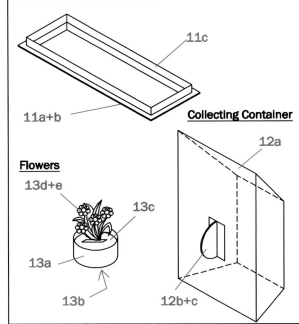

Collecting Container

Flowers

Bottle

- make a cylinder 14a
- make a cone 14b
- make a small cylinder 14c
- glue the three parts

Suitable Sand

To move the model you need fine sand, for example sand for bird cages. But be careful of the added pieces of lime. They could block the sand hopper's opening. Please sift them out before.

Function Test

Put sand into the hopper - it will trickle on the blue lever and the pianists arms will lift. Then the sand will slide down from the lever and the arms will lower again.
Attention: Don't forget to put the sand collecting container before.

Troubleshooting Guide

- If the mechanism is caught, a push with your finger will be helpful.
- If the lever remains in an angle because there is sand running in as running off continuously, please bend the lever a little bit.

Final Assembly

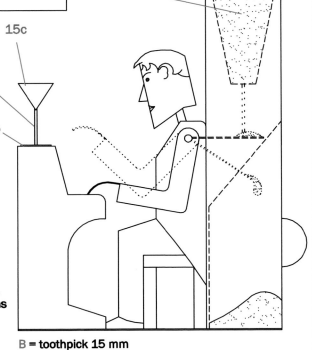

sifted sand

B = toothpick 15 mm

14. Gymnast

General Instructions:

⎯⎯⎯⎯⎯ continuous out-line: cut

⎯ ⎯ ⎯ ⎯ score and bend parts back (hill fold)

·············· score and bend parts forwards (valley fold)

—·—·— glue part

● glue (red dot)

⊠ cut out (red cross)

⊕ cut cross (black cross)

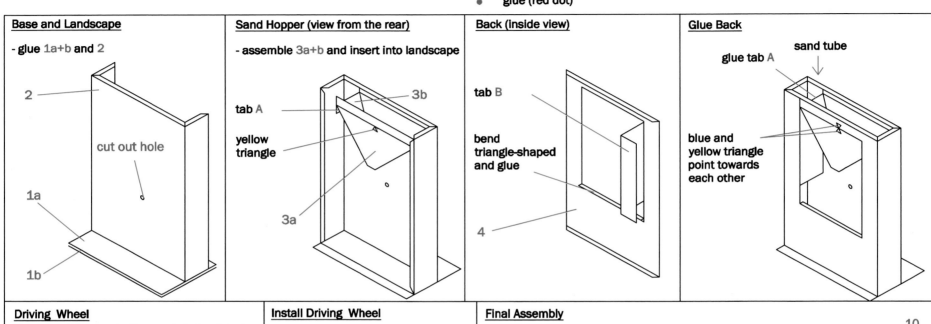

Base and Landscape

- glue 1a+b and 2

2

cut out hole

1a

1b

Sand Hopper (view from the rear)

- assemble 3a+b and insert into landscape

3b

tab A

yellow triangle

3a

Back (inside view)

tab B

bend triangle-shaped and glue

4

Glue Back

sand tube

glue tab A

blue and yellow triangle point towards each other

Driving Wheel

For assembling push discs on kebab stick, then remove stick. The wheel shouldn't wobble.

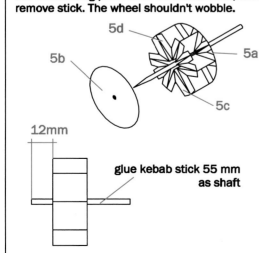

5d

5b

5a

5c

12mm

glue kebab stick 55 mm as shaft

Install Driving Wheel

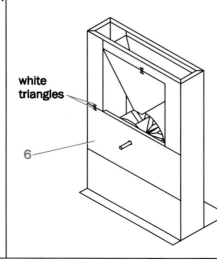

white triangles

6

Final Assembly

1. Glue washer 7 on shaft. The driving wheel should rotate smoothly
2. Assemble gymnast 8a-e and push on the kebab stick. Shoulder joint = 6mm toothpick
3. Glue support 9a-d on base 1. The horizontal bar mustn't rub.
4. Fill sand in the hopper, make a function test
5. Glue cover 10

Movement

To move the model you need fine sand, for example sifted sand for bird cages.

Turn the model and the sand will move in the sand tube and then into the hopper. From there the sand will trickle on the driving wheel and move the gymnast.

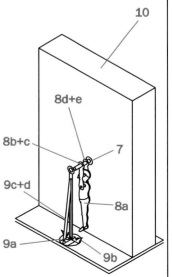

10

8d+e

8b+c

7

9c+d

8a

9a

9b

1. CRANK SLIDER   48

2. OSCILLATING LEVER   49

3. FRICTION TRANSFER   52–53

4. MESHING GEARWHEELS   56–57

5. RATCHET   57–60

6. CAMS & FRICTION WHEEL   61–64

7. CAM & PUSHROD   65–68

1

2

3

4

5

6

7

8. CAM & LEVER   69–72

9. HAPPY BIRTHDAY   64, 73

10. AT THE DUCK'S POND   76–80

11. PYRAMID LIFTER   81–85

12. THE WEIGHT OF
      BUREAUCRACY   88–93

13. PIANIST   96–100

14. GYMNAST   101–105

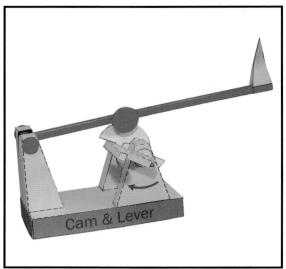

8

9

10

11

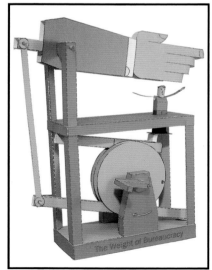

12

13

14

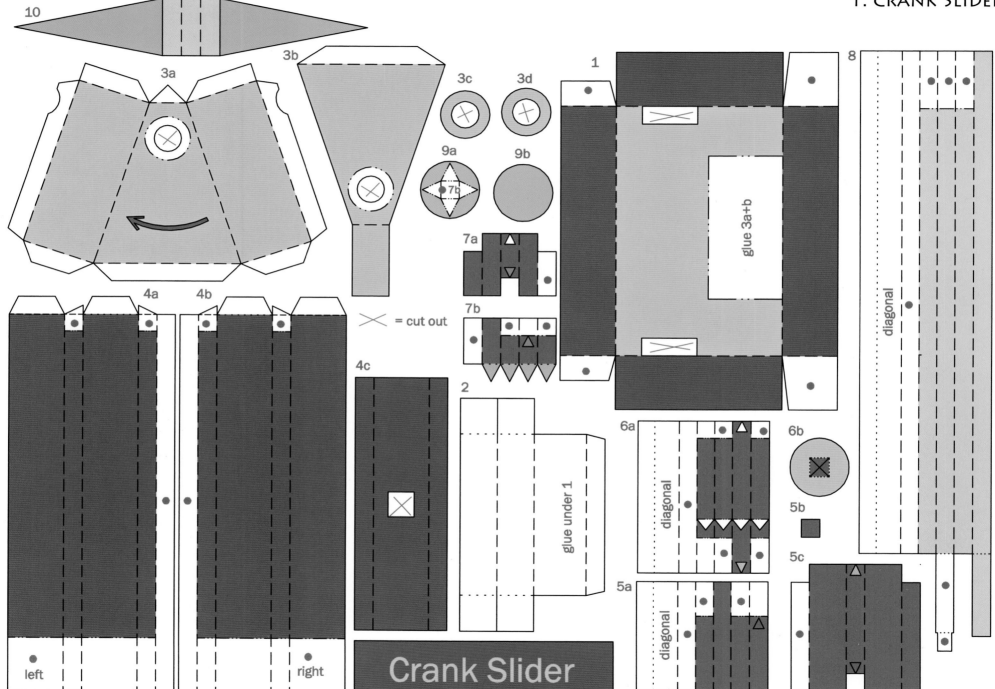

10

3a
3b
3c
3d

1
8

9a
9b
7b

7a

glue 3a+b

7b

✕ = cut out

4a
4b

4c

2

diagonal

6a
6b

5b

glue under 1

5c

5a

diagonal

diagonal

left
right

Crank Slider

48

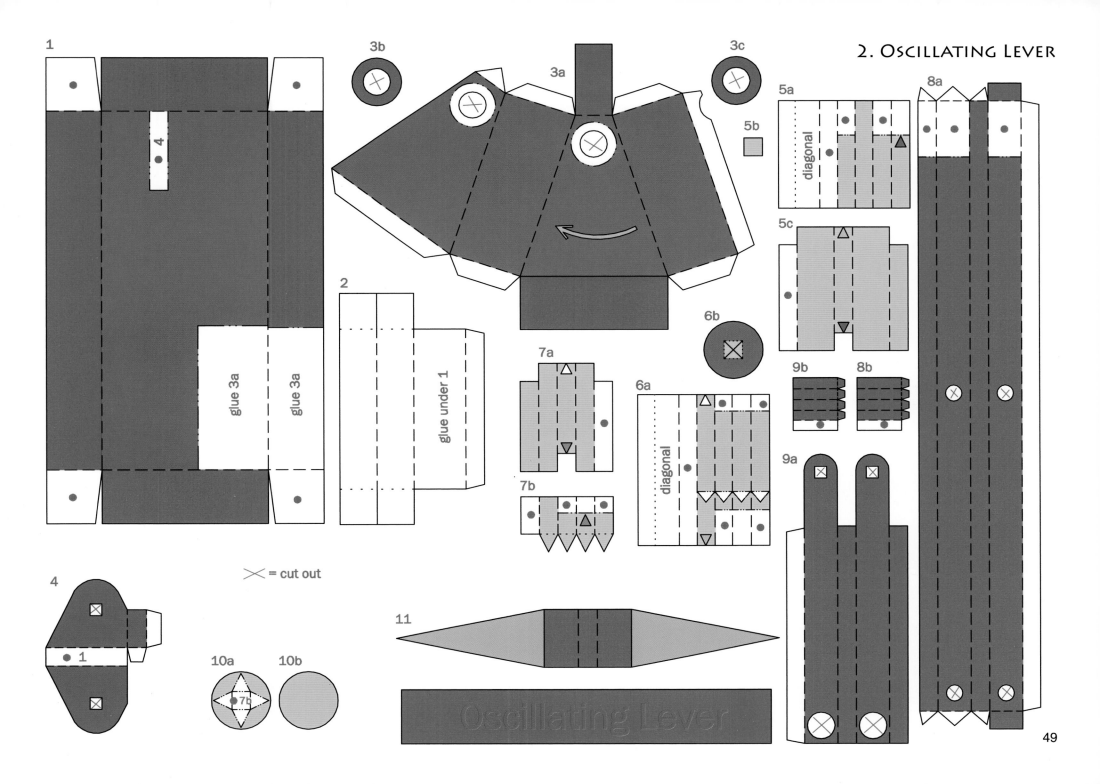

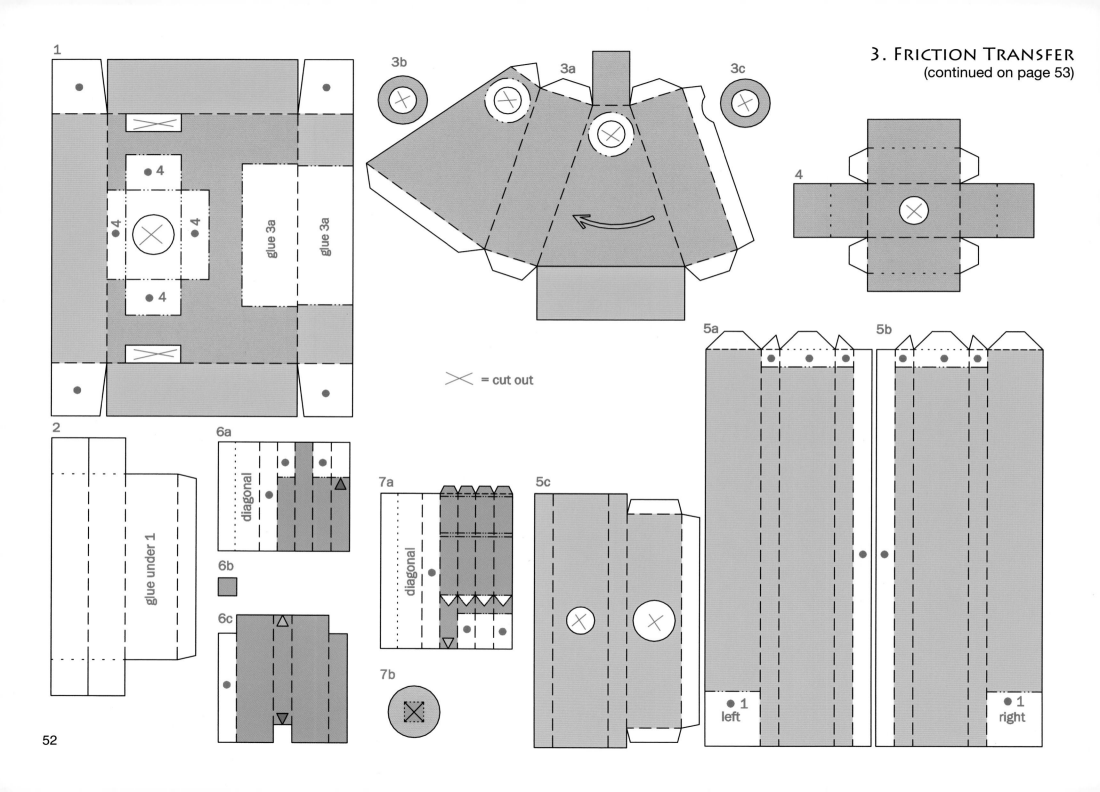

(continued on page 53)

1

4
4 4 4
4

glue 3a   glue 3a

3b
3a
3c
4

✕ = cut out

2

glue under 1

6a
diagonal

6b

6c

7a
diagonal

7b

5c

5a
5b

● 1
left

● 1
right

Friction Transfer

8d

9a

10a

9b

8a

8c

10b

11b

⊠ = cut out

8b

11a

8a

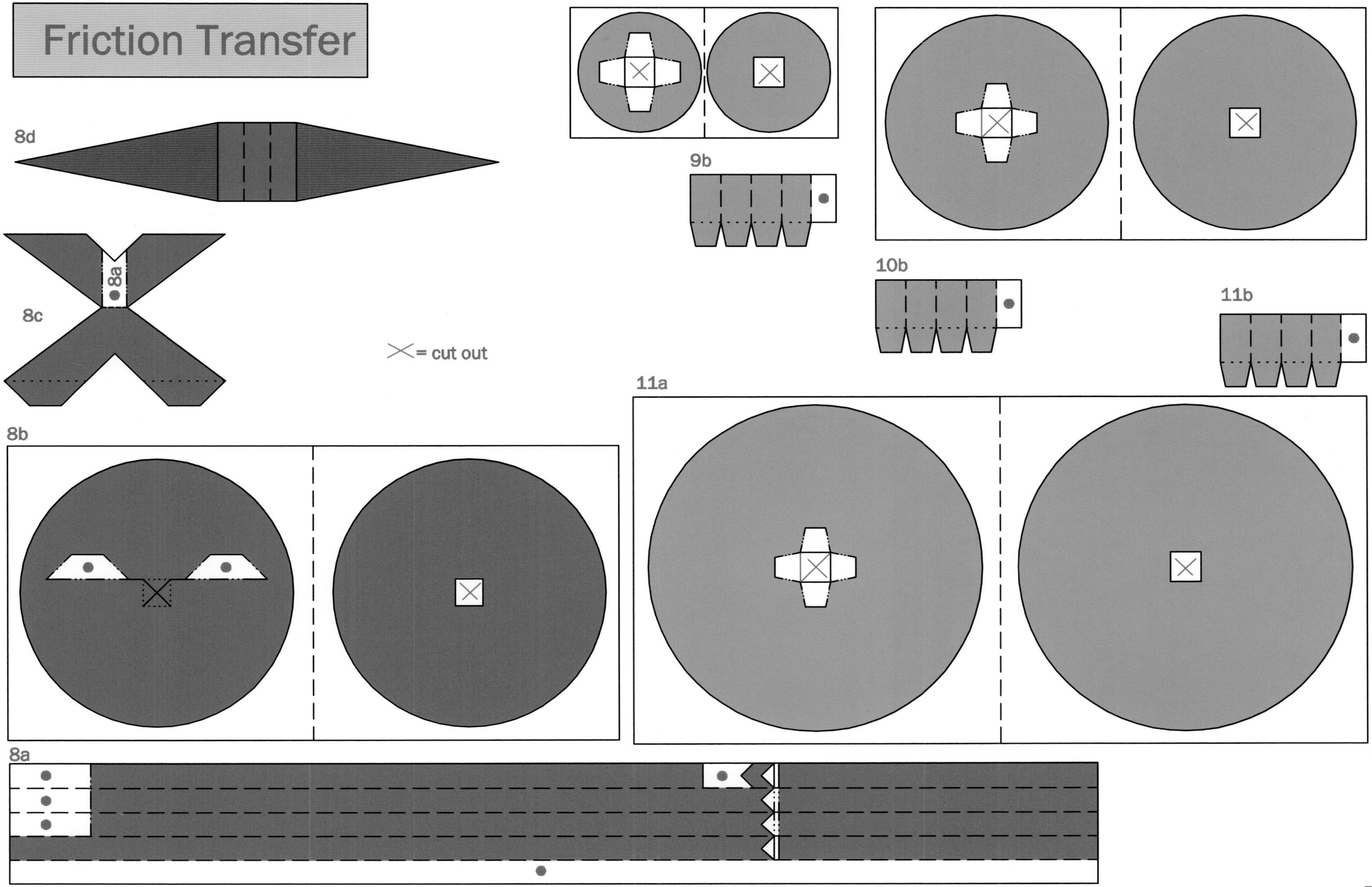

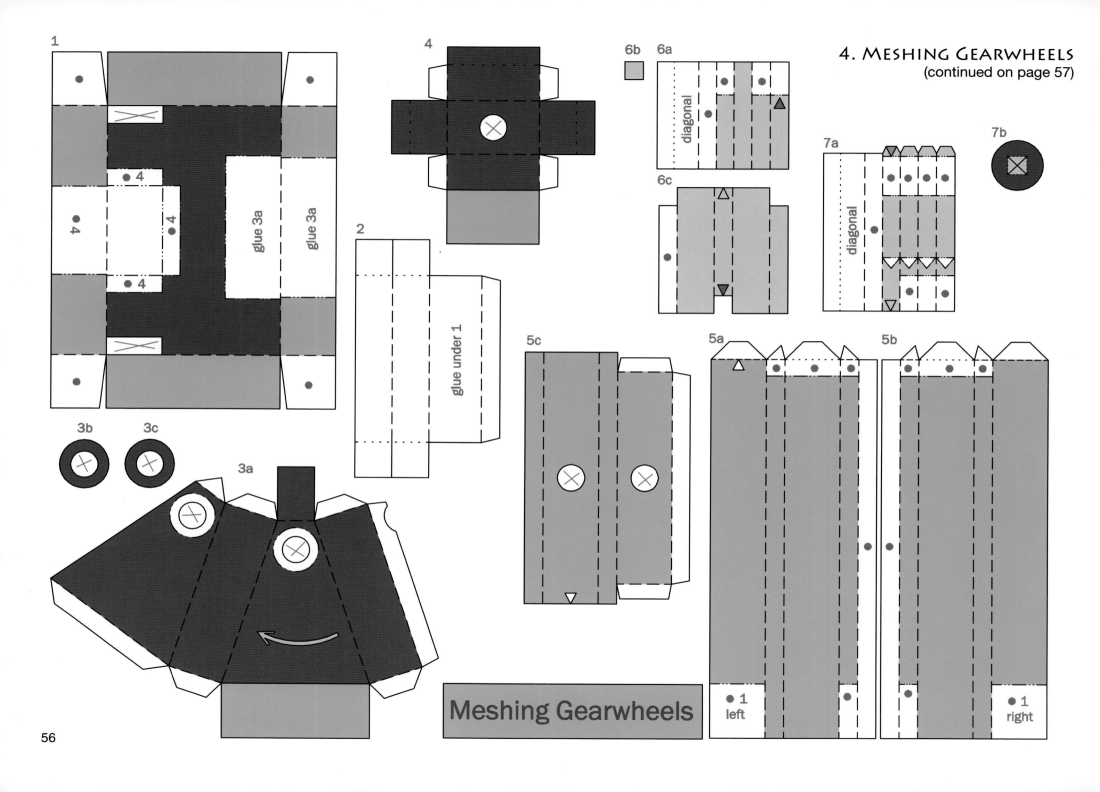

4. MESHING GEARWHEELS
(continued on page 57)

Meshing Gearwheels

4. MESHING GEARWHEELS
(continued from page 56)

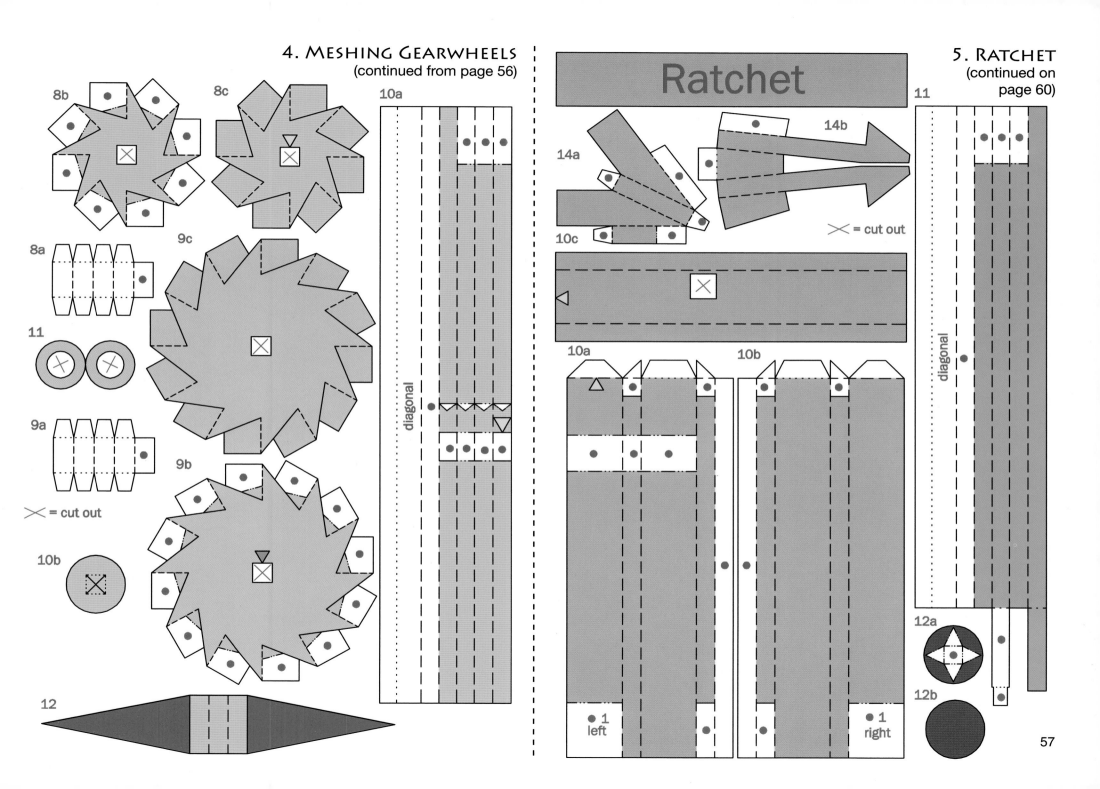

8b

8c

10a

8a

9c

11

9a

9b

✕ = cut out

10b

12

Ratchet

5. RATCHET
(continued on page 60)

14a

14b

10c

✕ = cut out

11

diagonal

10a

10b

diagonal

● 1 left

● 1 right

12a

12b

57

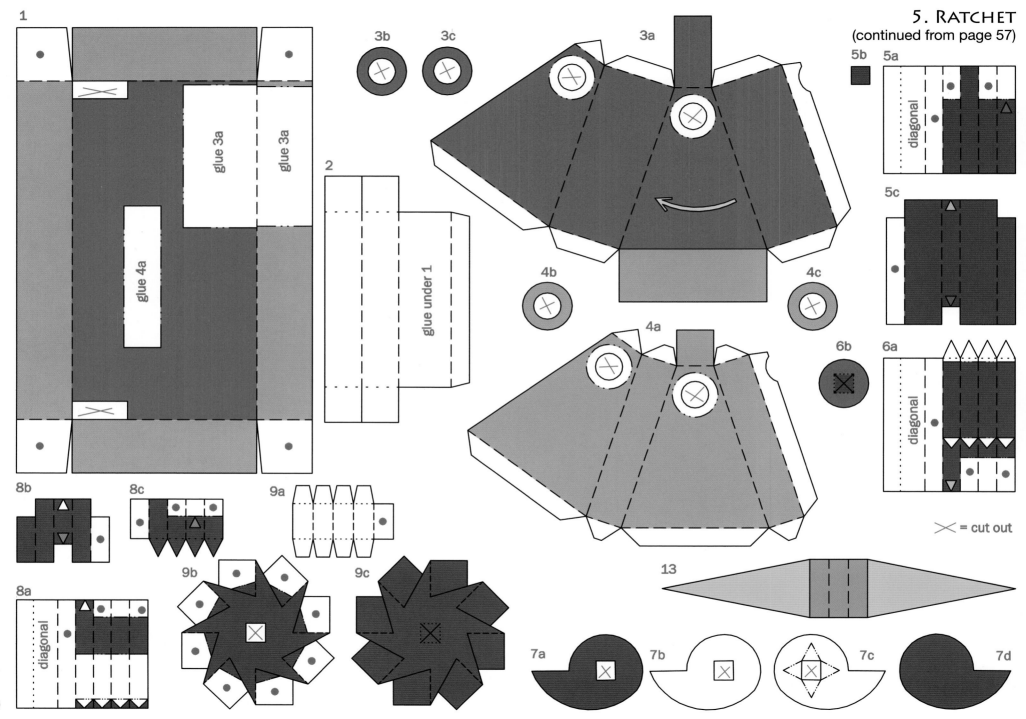

1

3b   3c

3a

5b   5a

2

glue 3a

glue 3a

glue 4a

glue under 1

diagonal

5c

4b   4c

6b   6a

4a

diagonal

✕ = cut out

8b   8c   9a

13

8a

9b   9c

7a   7b   7c   7d

diagonal

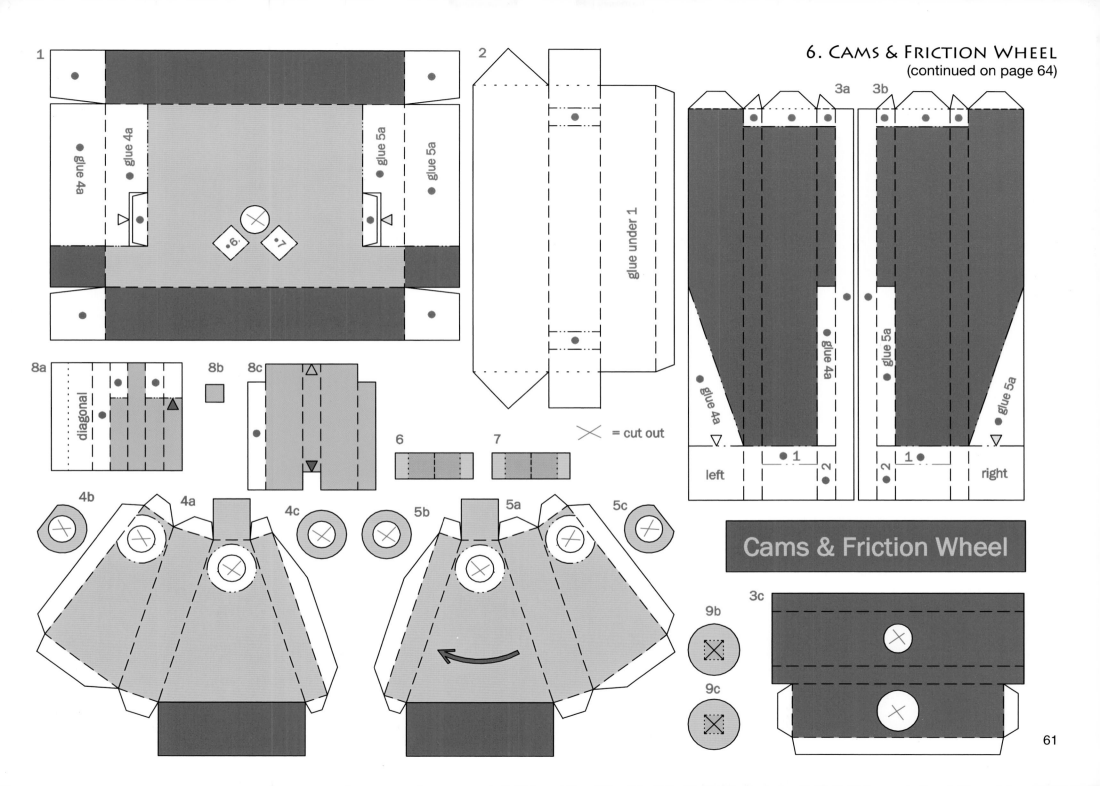

(continued on page 64)

1

glue 4a
● glue 4a
glue 5a
glue 5a

•6•
•7

2

glue under 1

3a   3b

glue 4a
● glue 4a
glue 5a
glue 4a
glue 5a

left   ● 1   2   2   1 ●   right

8a   diagonal   8b   8c

▽△

6   7   ✕ = cut out

4b   4a   4c   5b   5a   5c

Cams & Friction Wheel

3c

9b

9c

6. CAMS & FRICTION WHEEL
(continued from page 61)

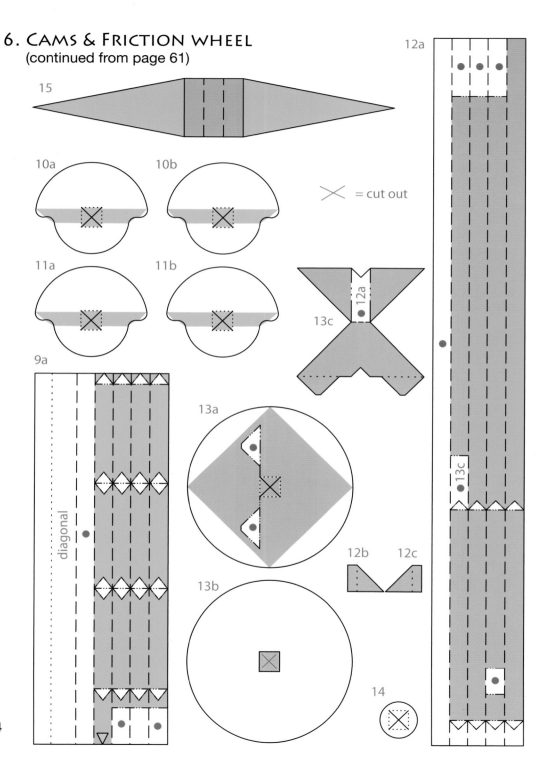

= cut out

9. HAPPY BIRTHDAY
(continued on page 73)

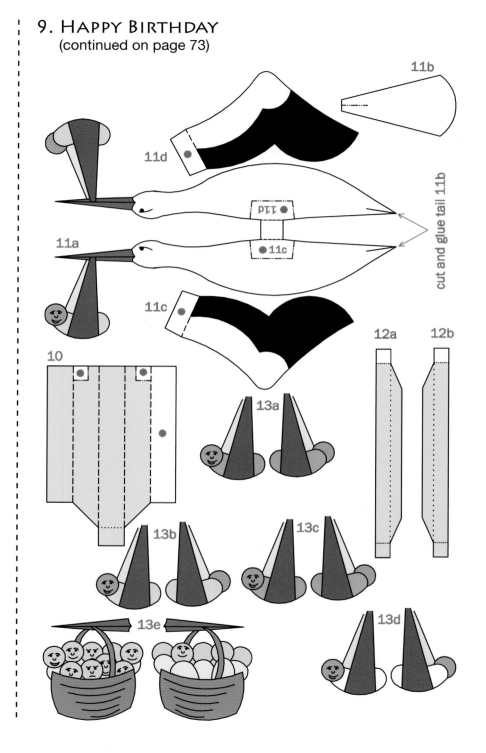

cut and glue tail 11b

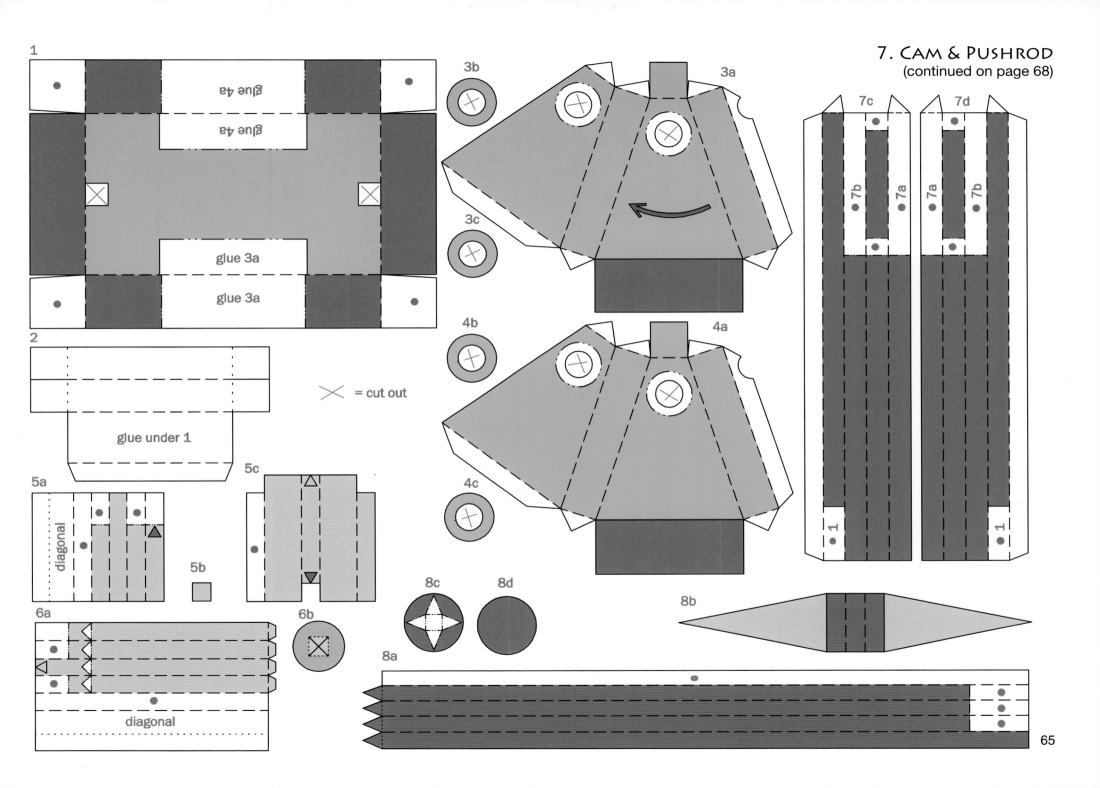

1

glue 4a

glue 4a

glue 3a

glue 3a

2

glue under 1

✕ = cut out

5a

diagonal

5b

5c

6a

diagonal

6b

3b

3a

3c

4b

4a

4c

7c

7d

7b

7a

7a

7b

1

1

8c

8d

8b

8a

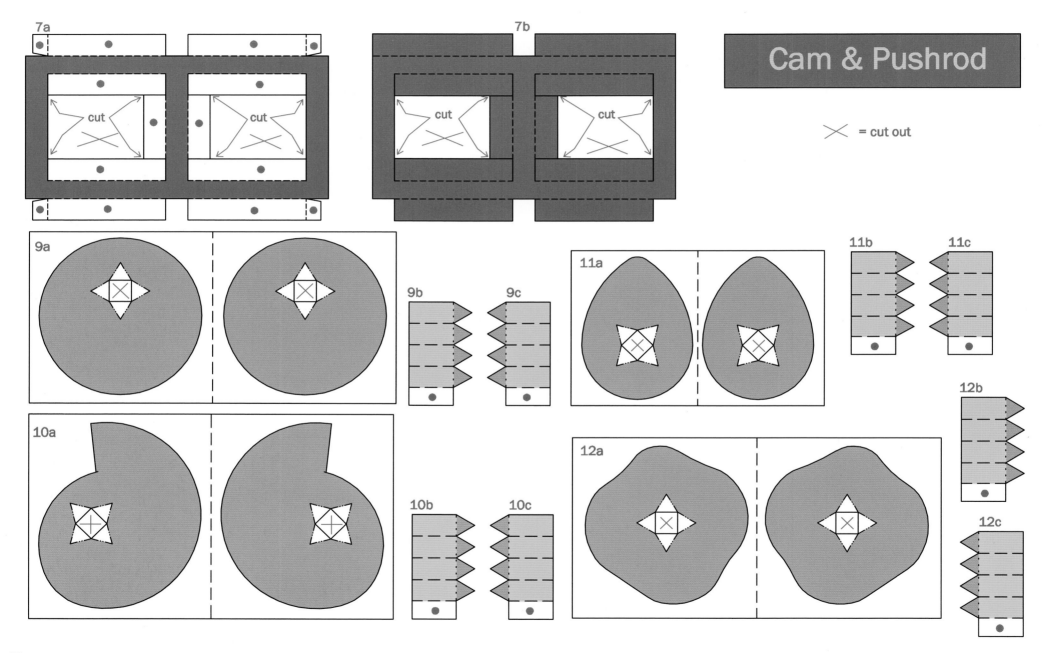

Cam & Pushrod

✕ = cut out

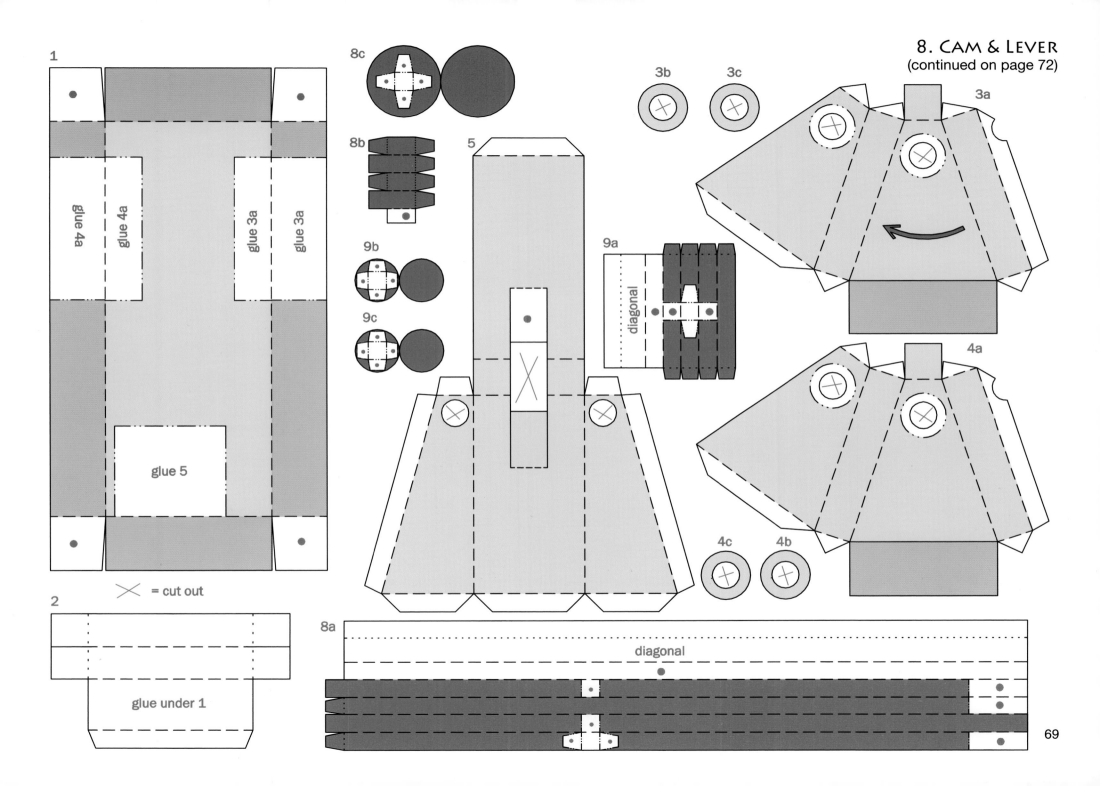

1

glue 4a

glue 4a

glue 3a

glue 3a

glue 5

8c

8b

9b

9c

5

9a

diagonal

3b

3c

3a

4a

4c

4b

✕ = cut out

2

glue under 1

8a

diagonal

Cam & Lever

14b

14c

14a

6a

diagonal

6c

7a

diagonal

7b

6b

13a

10

13b

13c

11a

11b

11c

$\times$ = cut out

12b

12c

12a

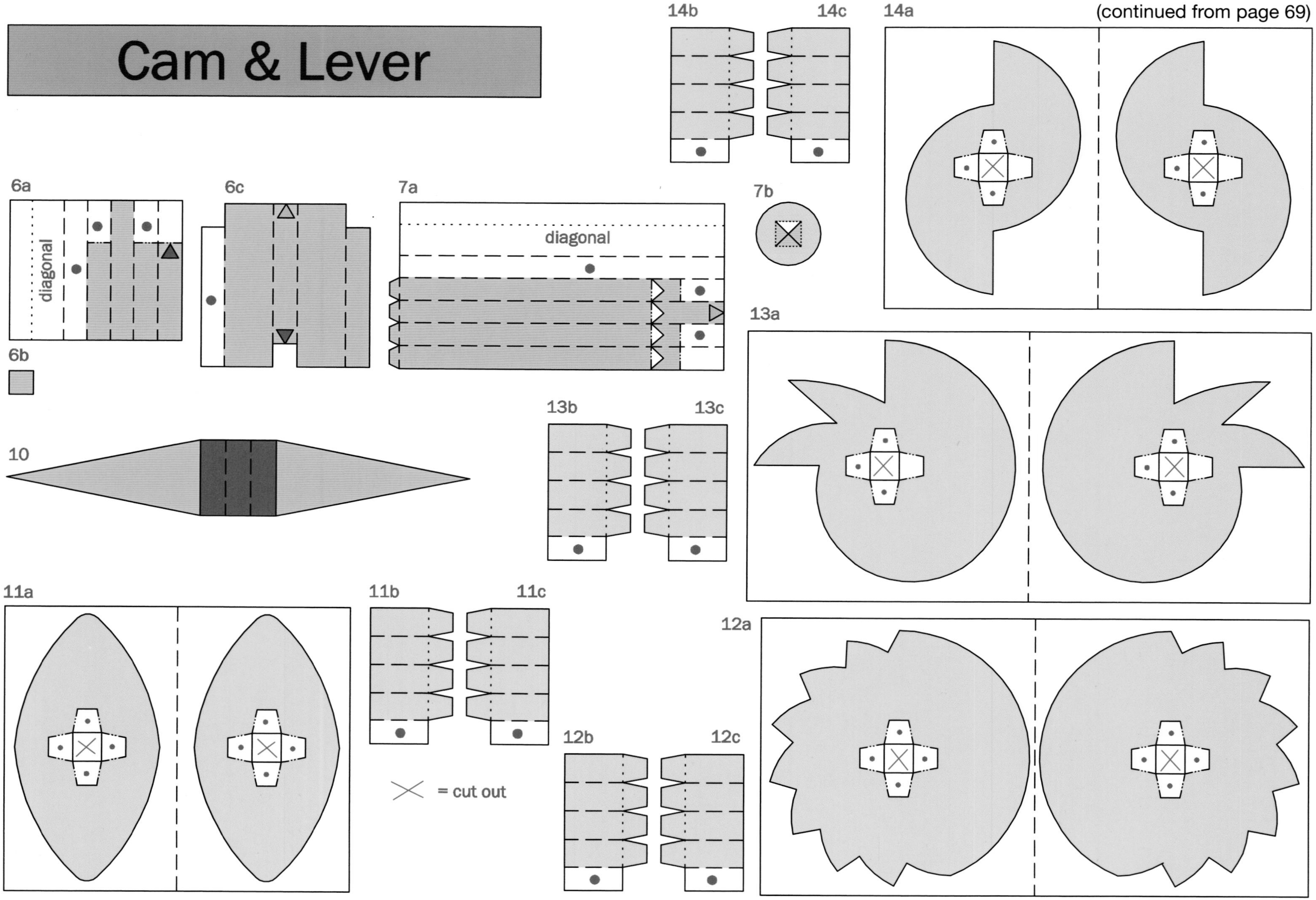

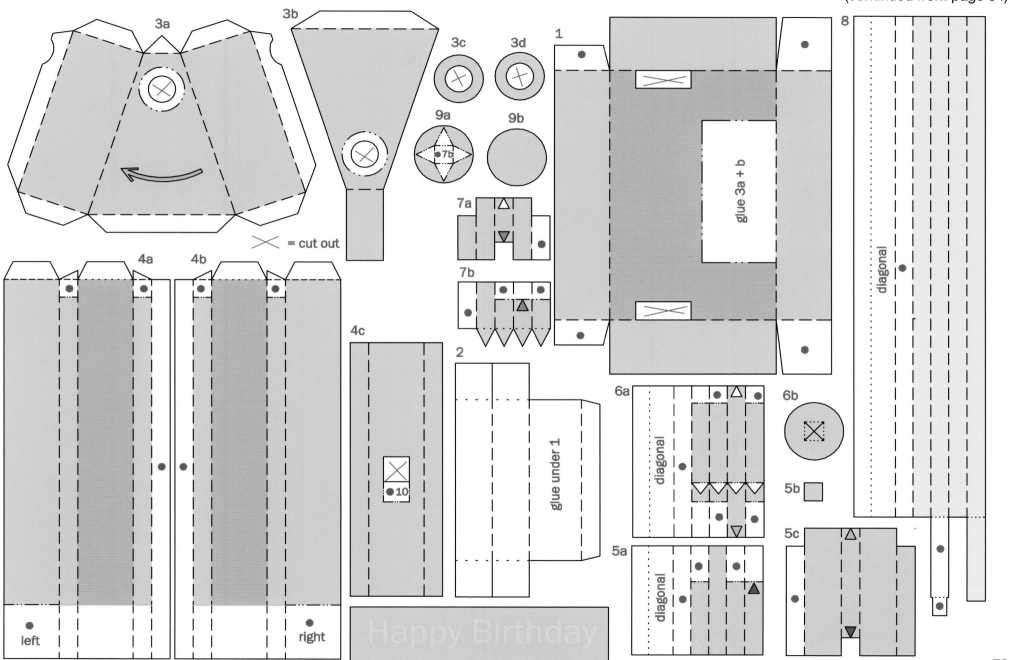

3a

3b

3c

3d

9a

9b

1

8

diagonal

glue 3a + b

$\times$ = cut out

7a

7b

4a

4b

4c

2

glue under 1

6a

diagonal

6b

5b

5c

5a

diagonal

10

left

right

Happy Birthday

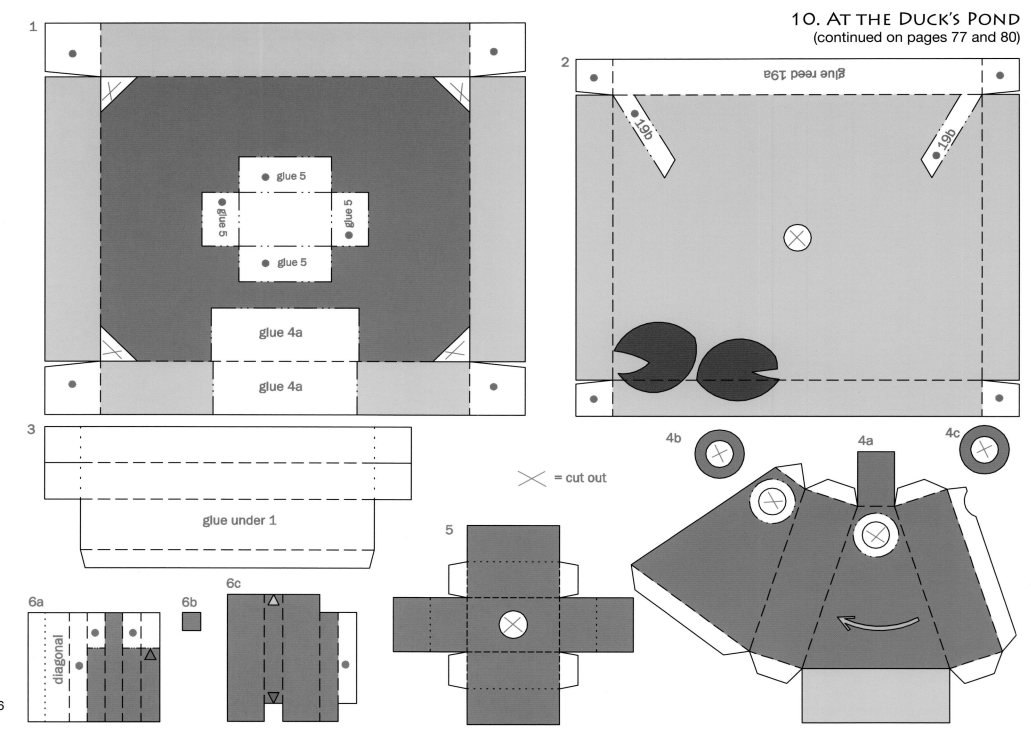

1

glue 5
glue 5
glue 5
glue 5

glue 4a

glue 4a

2

glue reed 19a

19b
19b

3

glue under 1

$\times$ = cut out

4b

4a

4c

5

6a

diagonal

6b

6c

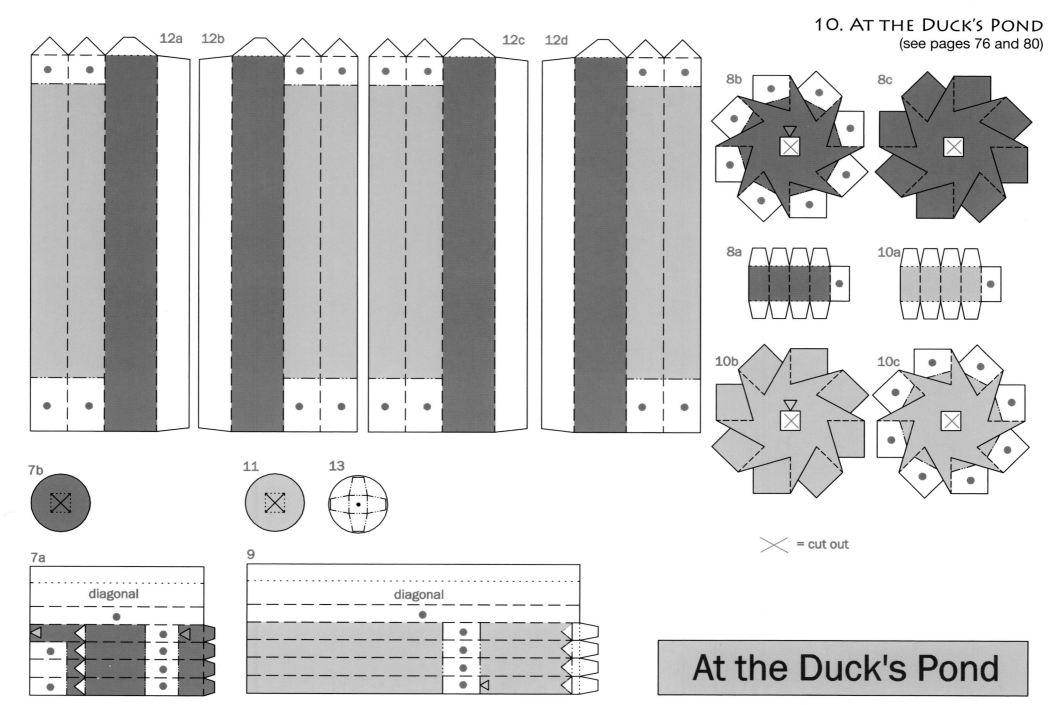

12a 12b 12c 12d

8b 8c

8a 10a

10b 10c

7b

11 13

✕ = cut out

7a

diagonal

9

diagonal

At the Duck's Pond

19b

19a

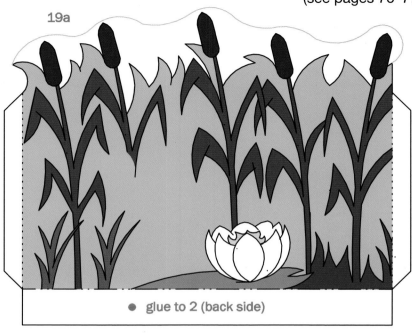

● glue to 2 (back side)

15a

21a   21b   20a   20b

15b

17a

16a

17b

18a

16b

18b

14

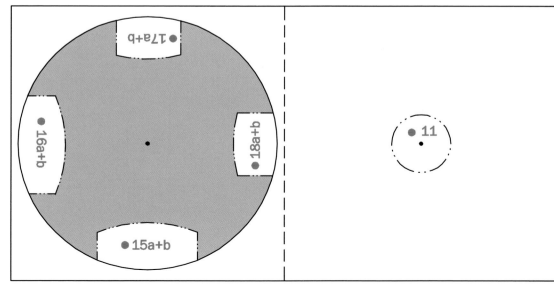

● 17a+b

● 16a+b

● 18a+b

● 11

● 15a+b

80

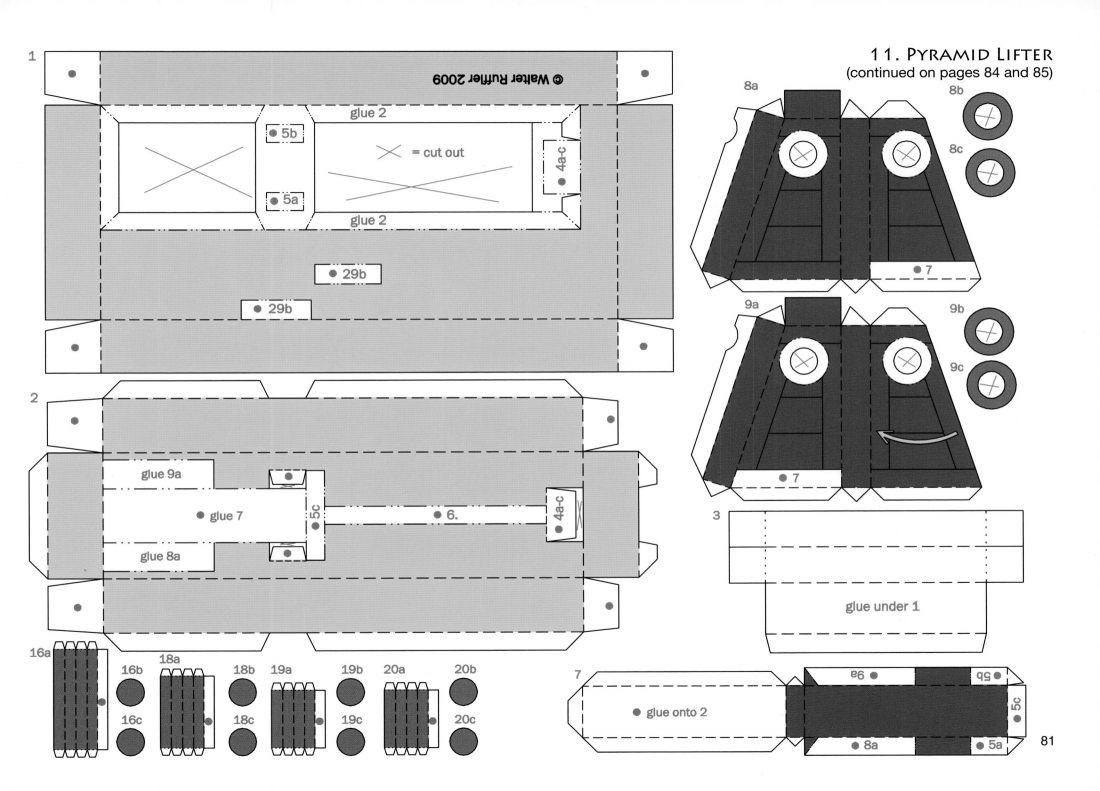

© Walter Ruffler 2009

glue 2

5b

× = cut out

4a-c

5a

glue 2

29b

29b

8a

8b

8c

7

9a

9b

9c

7

2

glue 9a

5c

glue 7

6.

4a-c

glue 8a

3

glue under 1

16a

16b

18a

18b

19a

19b

20a

20b

16c

18c

19c

20c

7

glue onto 2

9a

5b

5c

8a

5a

81

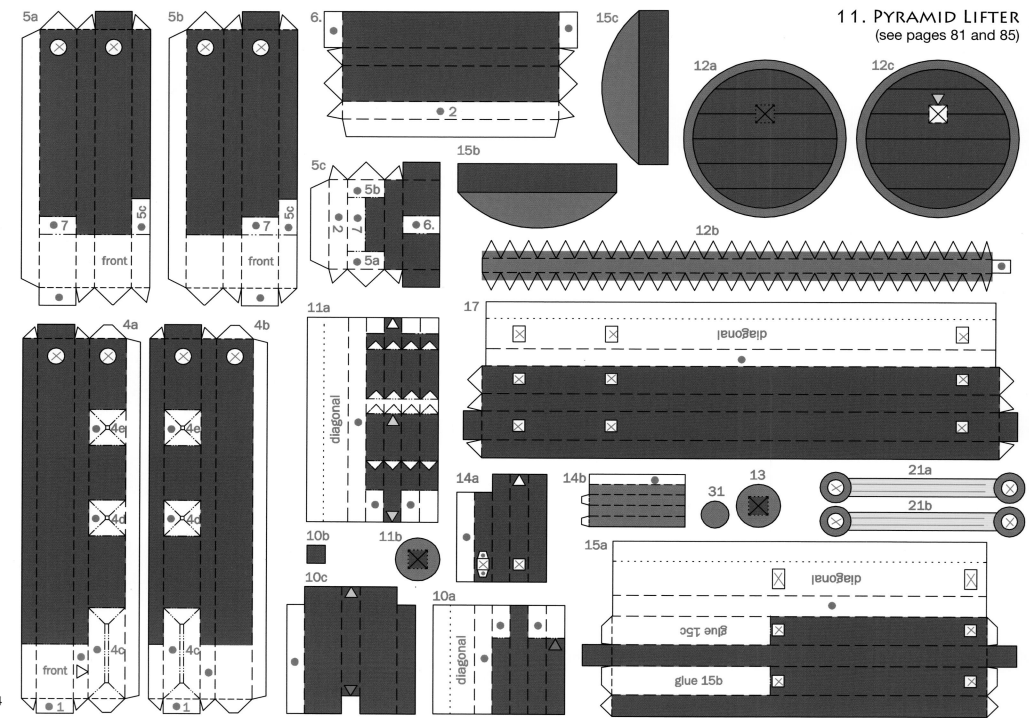

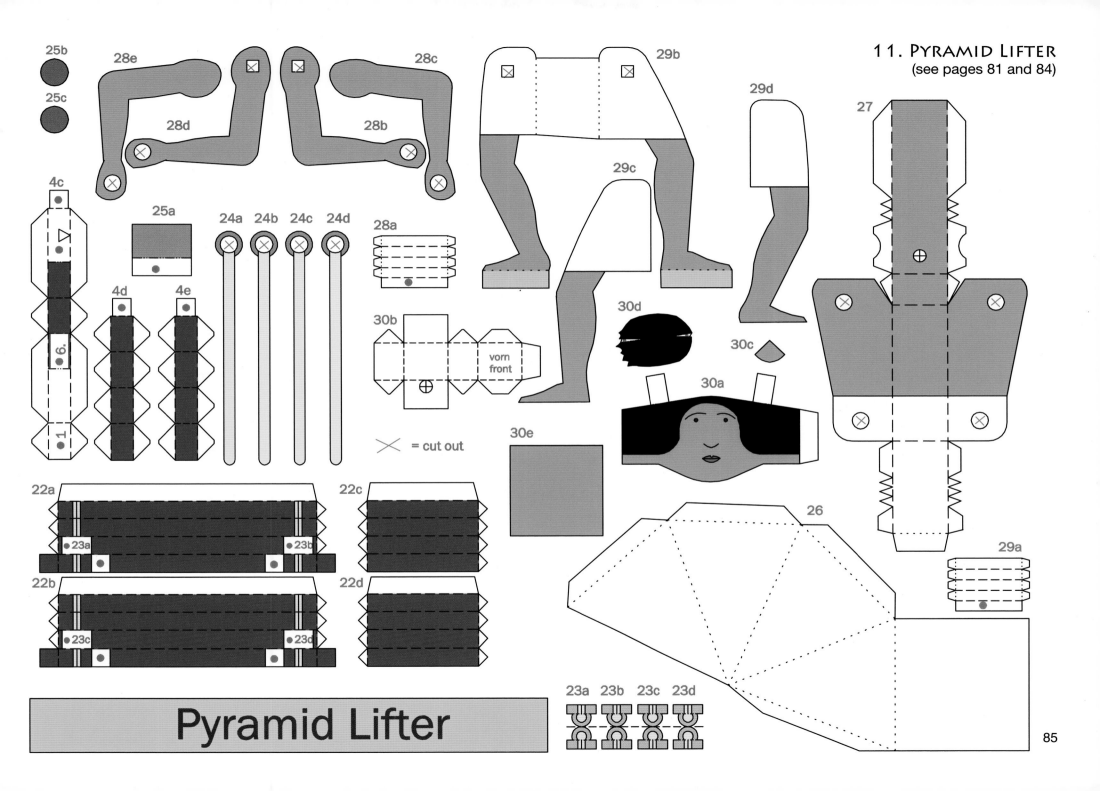

25b

25c

28e

28d

28c

28b

29b

29d

27

4c

25a

24a 24b 24c 24d

28a

29c

4d 4e

30b

vorn
front

30d

30c

30a

30e

✕ = cut out

22a

22c

• 23a

• 23b

22b

22d

• 23c

• 23d

26

29a

Pyramid Lifter

23a 23b 23c 23d

85

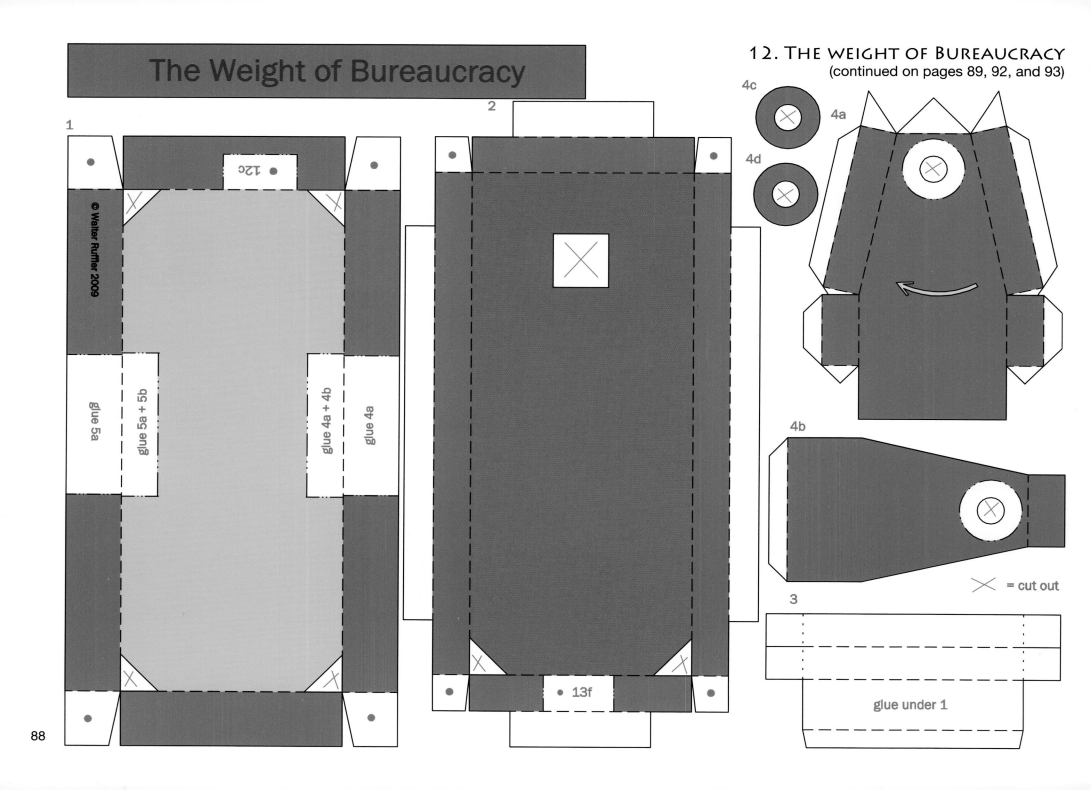

The Weight of Bureaucracy

© Walter Ruffler 2009

1

12c

glue 5a

glue 5a + 5b

glue 4a + 4b

glue 4a

2

13f

12. THE WEIGHT OF BUREAUCRACY
(continued on pages 89, 92, and 93)

4c

4a

4d

4b

= cut out

3

glue under 1

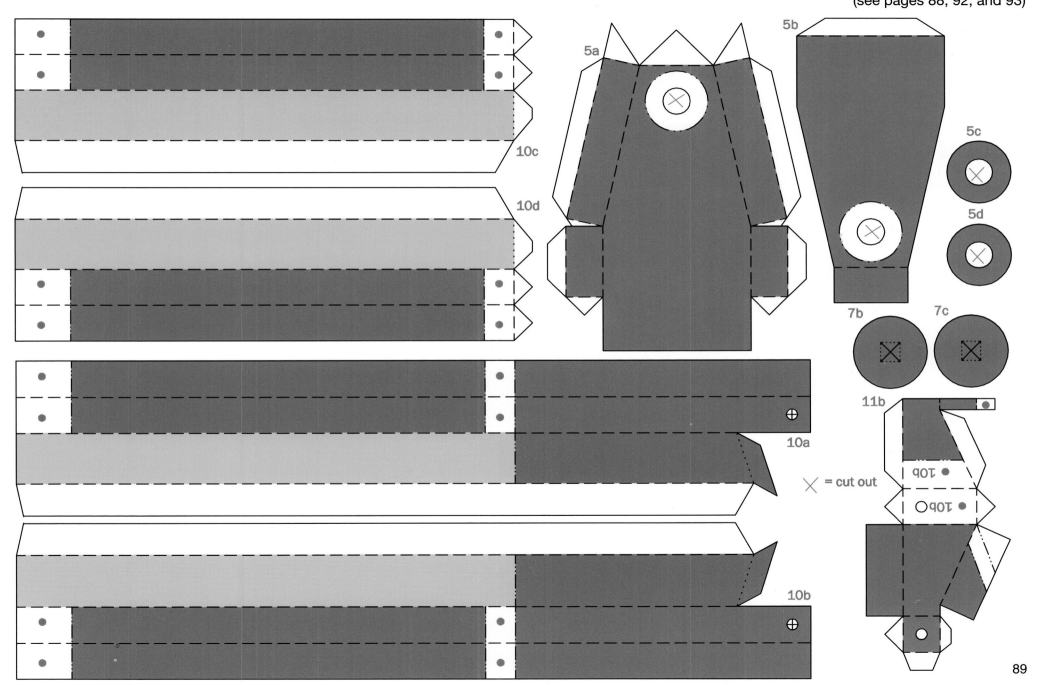

5a

5b

5c

5d

7b

7c

11b

10a

10b

10c

10d

10p

10p

✕ = cut out

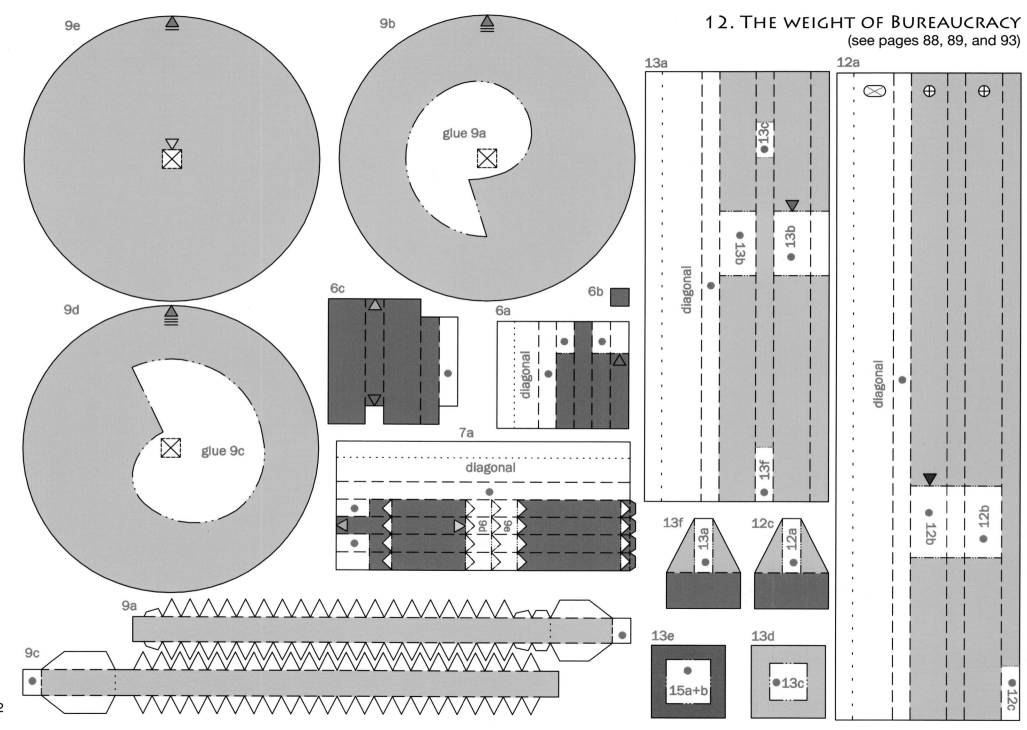

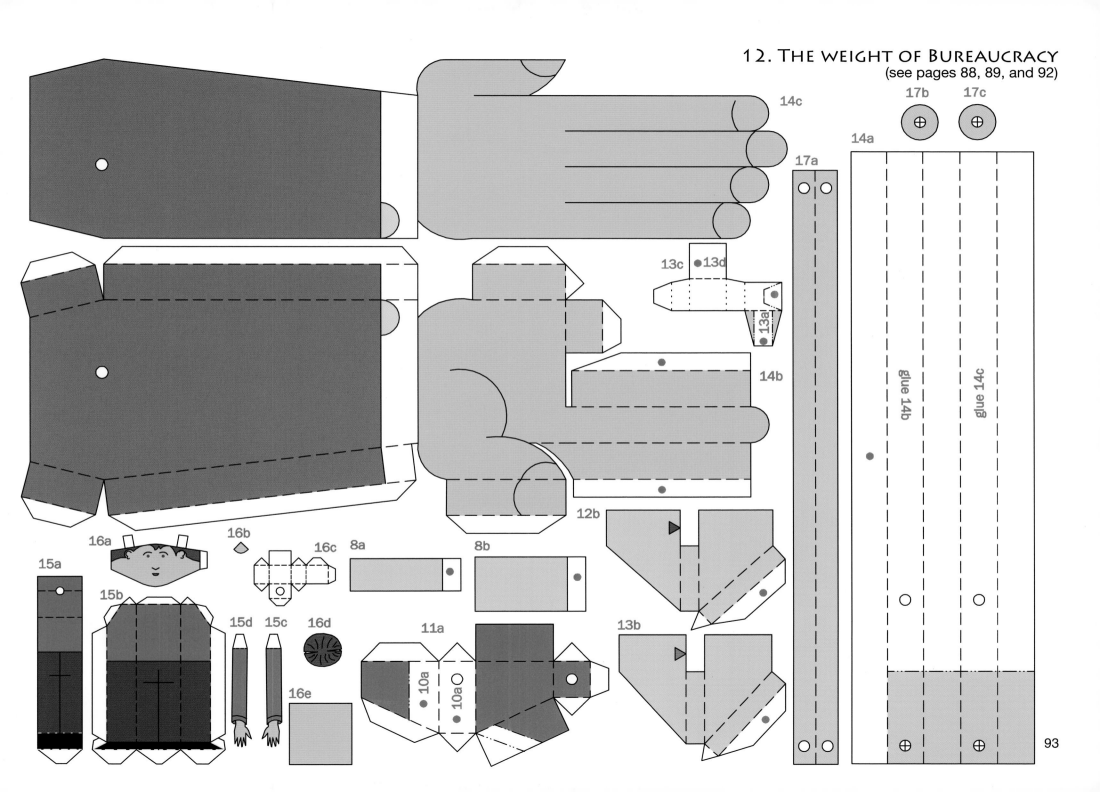

14c

17b   17c

14a

17a

13c 13d

13a

14b

glue 14b

glue 14c

16a   16b   16c   8a   8b

15a

15b   15d 15c   16d   11a

16e   10a   10a   13b

12b

93

(continued on pages 97 and 100)

2

1

6a

4

glue part 2

glue 5a+b

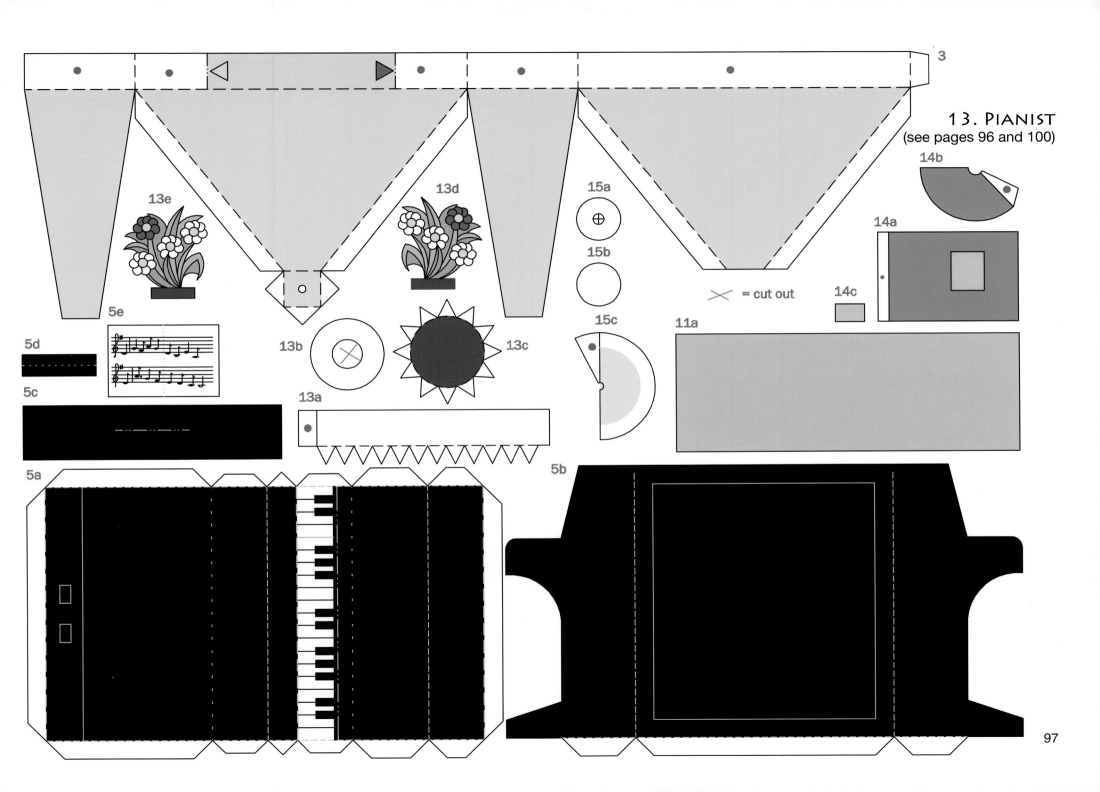

13. PIANIST
(see pages 96 and 100)

= cut out

97

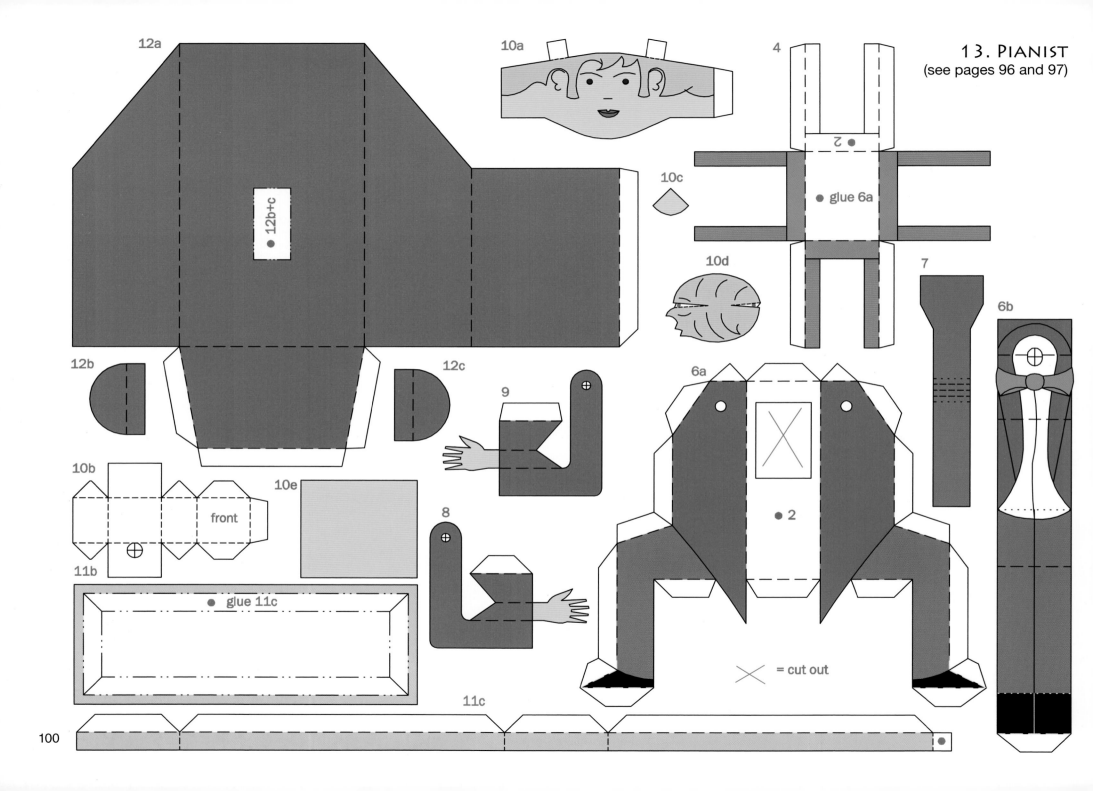

● 2

glue 4 ●

● glue 2

● 9b ● 9a

● 2

11

12

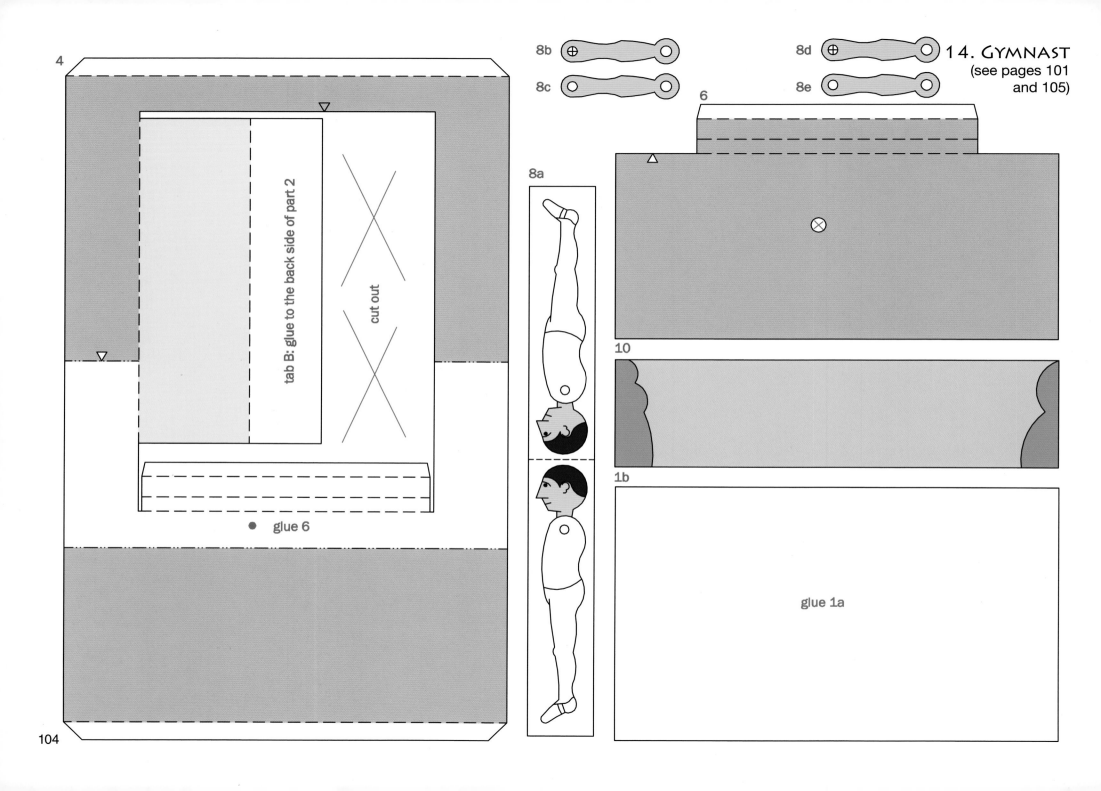

8b

8c

8d

8e

14. GYMNAST
(see pages 101 and 105)

4

tab B: glue to the back side of part 2

cut out

● glue 6

6

8a

10

1b

glue 1a

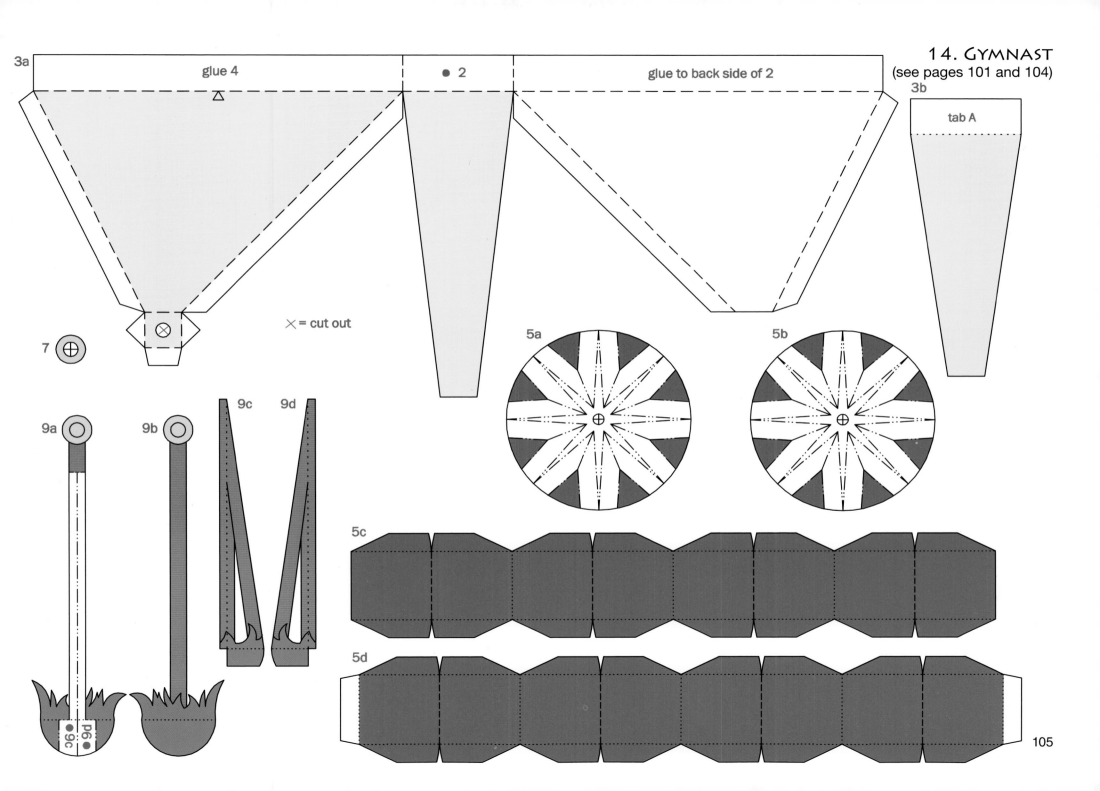

3a

glue 4

• 2

glue to back side of 2

3b

tab A

△

✕ = cut out

7 ⊕

5a

5b

9a

9b

9c

9d

5c

5d

p6
• 9c

THE AUTHOR

Walter Ruffler was born in 1949 in Algermissen, a village near Hanover in Germany. He studied philosophy, theology, German and political science. He has always been interested in drawing and sculpture and attended a great many courses, especially those in kinetic art, being particularly inspired by the Swiss artist Jean Tinguely. It was in 1999 that he first discovered the world of automata while attending a special exhibition in Switzerland put on by the British company 'Cabaret Mechanical Theatre'. This inspired him to start designing mechanical moving sculptures for himself. In his work he used many different materials but became especially intrigued by the possibilities of working in paper.

This book is the distillation of the methods and techniques that he has used and most of the photographs and models are of kits that he has designed himself. He now lives in Bremen and works as a teacher of technical drawing and technical mathematics at a vocational training centre. To date he has produced more than 25 kits of 'paper automata'.

For more information, please visit his website at www.walterruffler.de or contact him by email at WalterRuffler@aol.com

He would also like to thank Rob Ives and Magdalen Bear for allowing some of their automata to be included in this book.